D0140316

Managing Dyslexia
at University

Also available

Dyslexia: Surviving and Succeeding at College
Sylvia Moody
978-0-415-43058-6 (hbk)
978-0-415-43059-3 (pbk)
978-0-203-96130-8 (e-book)

Dyslexia at College
Dorothy Gilroy, T. R. Miles and Elizabeth Ann Du Pre
978-0-415-40417-4 (hbk)
978-0-415-40418-1 (pbk)
978-0-203-94479-0 (e-book)

Dyslexia and Inclusion: Classroom Approaches for Assessment, Teaching and Learning
Gavin Reid
978-1-84312-361-1 (pbk)

Day-to-Day Dyslexia in the Classroom
Rody Politt, Joy Pollock and Elisabeth Waller
978-0-415-33972-8 (pbk)

That's the Way I Think: Dyslexia and Dyspraxia Explained
David Grant
978-1-84312-375-0 (pbk)

Dyslexia: Action Plans for Successful Learning
Glynis Hannell
978-1-84312-214-2 (pbk)

Managing Asperger Syndrome at College and University: A resource for students, tutors and support services
Juliet Jamieson and Claire Jamieson
978-1-84312-183-1 (pbk)

Managing Dyslexia at University

A Resource for Students, Academic and Support Staff

**Claire Jamieson and
Ellen Morgan**

Routledge
Taylor & Francis Group

LONDON AND NEW YORK

First published 2008 by Routledge
2 Park Square, Milton Park, Abingdon, Oxon, OX14 4RN

Simultaneously published in the USA and Canada
by Routledge

270 Madison Ave, New York, NY 10016

Routledge is an imprint of the Taylor & Francis Group, an informa business

© 2008 Claire Jamieson and Ellen Morgan

Typeset in Adobe Garamond by FiSH Books, Enfield, Middx.
Printed and bound in Great Britain by TJ International Ltd, Padstow, Cornwall

Note: The right of Claire Jamieson and Ellen Morgan to be identified as the authors of this work
has been asserted by them in accordance with the Copyright, Designs and Patents Act 1988

All rights reserved. The purchase of this copyright material confers the right on the purchasing
institution to photocopy pages 71–87 only. No other part of this book may be reprinted or
reproduced or utilised in any form or by any electronic, mechanical, or other means, now known
or hereafter invented, including photocopying and recording, or in any information storage or
retrieval system, without permission in writing from the publishers.

British Library Cataloguing in Publication Data
A catalogue record for this book is available from the British Library

Library of Congress Cataloging in Publication Data
A catalog record for this book has been requested

ISBN 10: 1-84312-341-X
ISBN 13: 978-1-84312-341-5

A student's perspective

I was diagnosed as dyslexic shortly before I started university. I was nervous at the notion of going to university with this, a disorder that, for all I knew, could be some contagious tropical disease. It took me until after the first term to find the dyslexia service on the university website. From going to the one-to-one support sessions I started to find university not such an overwhelming place. During my support sessions, I got help with any aspect of work that I was finding difficult. Having the right type of support, without a doubt, still continues to make it possible to survive in a possibly threatening university environment. Understanding exactly what it is that you're finding difficult aids the tutor to pinpoint possible solutions during the tutorials. I now feel much more confident in tackling the academic demands on my course.

(*FG, psychology student*)

Contents

Foreword   xi
Preface   xiii
Acknowledgements   xiv
Abbreviations   xv

1   **Dyslexia**   1
    Audience: Academic staff, dyslexic students, disability staff, student welfare
    administration staff, students' union disability representatives
    What is dyslexia?   1
    Acquired dyslexia   1
    Developmental dyslexia   1
    Dyslexia and intelligence   3
    Dyslexia and spatial ability   3
    Dyslexia as a continuum: the interaction of causes and effects   3
    Late diagnosis   4
    Putting dyslexia in perspective   4
    Other specific learning difficulties   4
    Key points   7

2   **Assessment and Diagnosis of Dyslexia in Higher Education**   8
    Audience: dyslexic students and their parents or family members, disability staff,
    academic staff
    The DfES, now DIUS report 2005   8
    The diagnostic criteria for dyslexia   8
    IQ/attainment discrepancy   9
    Students with English as a second or additional language   10
    When is a reassessment necessary?   10
    What should be assessed?   11
    Which tests should be used?   11
    The assessment process   11
    The recommended format for a diagnostic assessment report   12
    Who is qualified to administer assessments?   12
    Routes to qualification   13
    The National Committee for Standards in Assessment, Training and Practice (informally
    known as SASC: SpLD Assessment Standards Committee)   13
    Funding and procedures for assessment   14
    The assessment report   14

Response to diagnosis 14

Benefits of assessment to previously undiagnosed students 15

Key points 16

3 Dyslexic Students in Higher Education 17

Audience: dyslexic students and academic staff

Students with an existing diagnosis 17

The changing profile of students in HE 18

Mature students 19

Choice of degree subject 19

Varying demands on literacy skills 20

Teaching and learning at university 20

Academic assessment at university 21

Marking the work of dyslexic students 21

The Association of Dyslexia Specialists in Higher Education (ADSHE) 22

Key points 23

4 Dyslexia within the Disability Framework 24

Audience: dyslexic students, disability/dyslexia staff, academic staff

The Disability Discrimination Act 1995 (DDA) 24

Dyslexia as a disability 26

The dyslexia 'label' 27

The Disabled Students' Allowances (DSA) 27

Key points 33

5 Dyslexia: Effects and Strategies 34

Audience: Academic staff, dyslexic students

Reading 34

Writing 37

Number skills 42

Oral Skills 43

Examinations 44

Foreign Languages 44

Time Management 45

Key points 47

6 Reasonable Adjustments 48

Audience: dyslexia/disability staff, academic staff, non-academic support staff, dyslexic students

Background information 48

Competence standards 48

Examples of reasonable adjustments 49

Placements 56

Students not in receipt of DSA funding 58

Key points 59

7   **Roles and Responsibilities**   60
    Audience: dyslexic students, academic staff, dyslexia tutors
    Models of dyslexia and disability services   60
    Accessing support   60
    Who is likely to provide what help?   62
    Responsibilities of the student   66
    International students   67
    Key points   68

CD and photocopiable resources   69
    Student registration document (dyslexia/disability services)   71
    Permission to disclose personal information   74
    Notification of student's registration as dyslexic   75
    Confidential information for academic/library staff   76
    Application for support from the HE Access to Learning Fund (ALF)   77
    ALF application (alternative form) 2   80
    Student questionnaire (screening/background to assessment)   82
    Dyslexia tuition record form   86
    Dyslexia tuition evaluation form   87

    References   88
    Websites   90
    Other resources   92
    Index   93

Foreword

Those of us working in Higher Education are privileged to be involved in an era in which the widening participation agenda has opened doors to many students who previously might have been denied entry. The university community now embraces students from a wide background and the diverse nature of the student body enhances the academic environment. However, this change in student population also presents challenges to staff who must be able to identify and meet the needs of new groups of students. One group who have previously been largely ignored in the Higher Education sector are students with disabilities.

New legislation in the UK has provided a legal framework to ensure that students with disabilities are granted equal access to all aspects of university life. Academic and support staff throughout the university must be able to implement reasonable adjustments to ensure that no student is denied the opportunity to enjoy all the benefits of higher education.

In my role as Dean of Students, I am aware of some of the struggles that dyslexic students have encountered in their attempts to succeed at university. I am also aware of the difficulties faced by academic staff who often feel at a loss in knowing how to accommodate the needs of students whose 'disability' is not visible, and is often not easily understood. Despite their willingness to make appropriate adjustments, staff often feel unsure what form these adjustments should take, and are frustrated by their own lack of knowledge about dyslexia.

Managing Dyslexia at University provides a straightforward approach to answering many of the questions and uncertainties relating to issues such as how to identify and diagnose dyslexia, what the likely impact of dyslexia is on a student's academic performance and how support staff and academic staff can adjust teaching and assessment practice in order to facilitate a successful and fulfilling university experience for dyslexic students.

This book is overdue and answers many questions relating to the support available to dyslexic students, including providing a clear account of the often confusing maze that students must navigate to access technological as well as specialist dyslexia support. It also explains the likely impact of dyslexia on a student's academic life and suggests many approaches to ensure that the dyslexic student is offered a level playing field with non-dyslexic peers. There are many helpful strategies for both students and their lecturers. The topics addressed in the book are presented within the context of the current legislation which underpins the institutional requirement to establish appropriate adjustments to meet the needs of the increasing numbers of dyslexic students at university.

There is little doubt that this book will serve as a valuable reference for dyslexic students, their parents, teachers and other university support staff, such as librarians, careers advisors and specialist staff working in dyslexia and disability units. It is a welcome addition to the existing literature on dyslexia.

Dr Malcolm Cross
PhD C.Psychol AFBPS
Head of Department of Psychology
Dean of Students
City University, London

Preface

There is no shortage of books about dyslexia. In the past thirty years, there has been a prolific output by academic psychologists, neuroscientists, teachers and a range of other professionals, and the number of publications on the subject continues to grow. For anyone wanting to study the cognitive bases of dyslexia and its manifestations across the age range, there is a large number of volumes from which to choose. For specialist teachers of dyslexic children or students, there are very good books on methods for teaching literacy and study skills.

What then, is the purpose of yet another book about dyslexia? Dyslexic students who are going through the university application process and embarking on their degree courses seem to be bombarded with information and instructions from countless sources about procedures for disabled students. While they may be relieved to know that at this stage of their education they are likely to be well supported, in terms of technical assistance, tuition and assessment arrangements, students may be unsure about how universities organise their dyslexia services, whom they should tell about their dyslexia and whether and at what stage they should mention their dyslexia to their tutors. It is hoped that in this small book students will be able to find answers to the many questions they may have about managing their dyslexia at university. The book may also be useful for parents of dyslexic students who have frequently acted as advocates for their dyslexic children and want some assurance that appropriate support will continue to be available at university.

Managing Dyslexia at University is not just for students and their families though. Our experience as dyslexia coordinators at universities has shown that academic teaching staff are often at a loss as to how they can support dyslexic students in their departments. What advice can personal tutors give to their students? What 'reasonable adjustments' should they make to their teaching and assessment process? In what way can they help their students to develop effective study-skills strategies? We hope to provide answers to these and other questions raised by those people who form a crucial part of the education of all students but who have largely been ignored in previous publications. Chapter 5, which covers the effects of dyslexia and ideas for developing effective study strategies, may be of particular interest to academic tutors as well as to dyslexic students.

Some of the information presented here will also be of interest to disability staff, specialist dyslexia staff and non-specialist staff such as librarians, examinations officers and departmental administrators, all of whom have an impact on making universities more manageable places for dyslexic students. This is a book to dip into rather than read from cover to cover. To facilitate this, we have provided summaries for each chapter and a detailed index for cross-referencing and we have identified information which might be of particular interest to specific groups of people at various points throughout the book. In the contents section and at the beginning of each chapter, the likely audience is suggested.

Photocopiable resources, which can be customised for use by disability and dyslexia staff, can be found at the end of the book and on the CD.

Acknowledgements

We would like to thank a number of people who have helped us in various ways while working on this book. We are grateful to our colleagues in the disability centres at our respective universities: Andrea Kenneally and Sheila Blankfield from City University, and Marion Hingston Lamb and Jenny O'Sullivan from University College London (UCL). They helped us to identify the information about dyslexic people that would be most useful to our readers, and they have given us valuable feedback on the manuscript. We are also grateful to academic staff from several departments who have aired their concerns about the management of dyslexia at Higher Education (HE) level and have motivated us to produce this resource. In particular, Sarah Simpson from the Department of Human Communication Science, UCL was always happy to discuss our ideas. We also owe thanks to countless students from City University and UCL, some of whose reflections we have quoted. Last but not least, a big 'thank you' to Wally Morgan, who was extremely generous in his support and encouragement throughout.

Abbreviations

ADSHE	Association of Dyslexia Specialists in Higher Education
ALF	Access to Learning Fund
AMBDA	Associate Member of the British Dyslexia Association
APE	Accreditation of Prior Experience
APL	Accreditation of Prior Learning
BDA	British Dyslexia Association
BPS	British Psychological Society
CPD	Continuing Professional Development
DA	Dyslexia Action (formerly DI, Dyslexia Institute)
DCSF	Department for Children, Schools and Families (formerly DfES, Department for Education and Skills)
DDA	Disability Discrimination Act
DED	Disability Equality Duty
DIUS	Department for Innovation, Universities and Skills (formerly DfES, Department for Education and Skills)
DRC	Disability Rights Commission
DSA	Disabled Students' Allowances
EAL	English as an Additional Language
ESOL	English for Speakers of Other Languages
HADC	Helen Arkell Dyslexia Centre
HEFCE	Higher Education Funding Council for England
HESA	Higher Education Statistics Agency
IDA	International Dyslexia Association
LA	Local Authority
LLLU+	London Language and Literacy Unit
NFAC	National Federation of Access Centres

NHS-SGU	National Health Service-Student Grants Unit
NVQ	National Vocational Qualification
OU	Open University
PATOSS	Professional Association for Teachers of Learners with Specific Learning Difficulties
QAA	Quality Assurance Agency
QAG	Quality Assurance Group
SASC	National Committee for Standards in SpLD Assessment Training and Practice
SEN	Special Educational Needs
SENDA	Special Educational Needs Disability Act (Part IV of the DDA)
SLC	Student Loan Company
SpLD	Specific Learning Difficulties
SSS	Scotopic Sensitivity Syndrome (also known as Meares-Irlen Syndrome, or Irlen Syndrome)
UCAS	University and Colleges Admissions Service

1

Dyslexia

AUDIENCE Academic staff, dyslexic students, disability staff, student welfare administration staff, students' union disability representatives

What is dyslexia?

There is much confusion as to what dyslexia is. Not only has understanding of the disorder developed and changed over more than 100 years but there are still differing theoretical views. It may seem that dyslexia quite simply defies definition. However, there are some things we can say with certainty. First, developmental dyslexia has a genetic and neurological basis (Smith et al. 1983, Grikorenko et al. 1997, Defries et al. 1997). Although the genetic basis is not yet fully understood, it is known that dyslexia is familial, that it runs in families. Second, it has been widely accepted for over twenty years that a key area of weakness in dyslexia is related to a particular aspect of language-processing, namely the processing of speech sounds (Bradley and Bryant 1983, Stanovich 1986). There is a strong relationship between the awareness of speech sounds and success in learning to read (Goswami and Bryant 1990, Snowling and Hulme 1994, Muter 2003), and there is evidence that a weakness in this area leads to problems in the acquisition of literacy skills, especially in languages whose writing system involves relating sounds to symbols. Third, it is now generally accepted that there is no relationship between dyslexia and general intelligence: dyslexia exists along the intellectual spectrum (see below).

Acquired dyslexia

The subject of this book is developmental dyslexia, a specific learning difficulty (SpLD) with a genetic basis. It should be distinguished from certain types of problems which may arise as a result of an insult to the brain due to a stroke or accident, which may manifest a range of different effects on receptive and expressive language and on both reading and writing. Studies that relate the area of damage to the brain with these effects cast light on the cognitive processes that underpin language and literacy. Difficulties of this nature are known as acquired dyslexia. While cognitive neuropsychological research into the effects of brain damage on reading and spelling informed early research into developmental dyslexia, the loss of pre-existing skills gives rise to very different patterns of behaviour in reading and writing.

Developmental dyslexia

If one is dyslexic, one is dyslexic from birth and will remain dyslexic (Pennington et al. 1990). This does not mean that the *effects* of dyslexia remain the same throughout life. Depending on a wide range of factors, not least getting older and more knowledgeable, the effects change constantly and, in many cases, become less problematic. But it is not possible to 'become' dyslexic – for example, on entering secondary school or university – just as it is not possible to stop being dyslexic on leaving school.

It would be difficult to improve on the definition of dyslexia adopted by the Board of Directors of the International Dyslexia Association in 2002:

> Dyslexia is a specific learning disability that is neurological in origin. It is characterised by difficulties with accurate and/or fluent word recognition and by poor spelling and decoding abilities. These difficulties typically result from a deficit in the phonological component of language that is often unexpected in relation to other cognitive abilities and the provision of effective classroom instruction. Secondary consequences may include problems in reading comprehension and reduced reading experience that can impede the growth of vocabulary and background knowledge.

(<http://www.interdys.org>)

There is also a strong association between dyslexia and deficits in short-term, or working, memory (Hulme et al. 1995 and Pickering 2000, cited in Mortimore 2003). Weakness in working memory has significant effects on a range of study skills, such as note-taking in lectures and processing text (see Chapter 5). Rote learning of, for example, multiplication tables, and sequences such as the alphabet or the months of the year are often very challenging and sometimes never mastered.

The phonological component of language relates to the sounds that make up words. In order to learn to read and write, it is necessary, in most languages, to be aware of speech sounds. At first, in small children, this awareness is not explicit, but even children as young as two or three are sensitive to rhyme, for example. They can recognise and generate sequences of words or nonsense words that rhyme. Children also become aware early in their speech and language development of the initial consonants in words. Once instruction in reading and writing begins, awareness of speech sounds, and particularly awareness of the individual sounds (phonemes) that make up words, needs to become more explicit. There is a reciprocal relationship between the development of literacy skills and the development of phonological awareness.

Children who do not have a natural propensity to develop effective phonological processing skills encounter problems in the initial stages of learning to read and write, because an essential building block is the association between speech sounds and the letters that are used to represent them in writing (Byrne 1998). Such children are often later identified as dyslexic, although appropriate intervention at an early age may be effective in overcoming obstacles to learning to read and write.

As dyslexia initially affects children's ability to identify the correspondence between letters and sounds, they have difficulty reading new words and may not be able to attempt to write words based on the way they sound. Dyslexic university students often remember having had great difficulty with 'phonics' at school; breaking words down to decode them for reading was a real struggle, and as far as spelling was concerned, it was often just a matter of guesswork based on visual memory, 'I'm sure it's got a "u" in it somewhere, but I'm not sure where'. The compensatory strategy most often used for poor decoding skills is to build up a large number of words which can be recognised at sight (sight vocabulary). Learners who do this successfully can often mask the effects of dyslexia, to the extent that it can remain unidentified, sometimes permanently and sometimes until they face the additional challenges of studying at degree level or even at post-graduate level.

Dyslexia and intelligence

Until relatively recently, diagnoses of dyslexia were based on a discrepancy between levels of attainment in literacy skills and underlying ability, or general intelligence. Learners whose reading and writing skills were surprisingly weak in relation to their other abilities could be identified as dyslexic, whereas those whose literacy skills were behind but more or less in line with their intelligence as measured by IQ tests were considered to have more general learning difficulties but not dyslexia. There has now been a move away from this position (Stanovich and Stanovich 1997, Fredrickson and Reason 1999, Siegel 1999).

When a core cognitive weakness, usually in phonological processing, is identified, and when this deficit affects the development of literacy skills, a diagnosis of dyslexia can be made regardless of IQ, assuming that IQ scores are within the 'normal' or average range. For more discussion about this issue, with particular reference to university students, see Chapter 2.

Dyslexia and spatial ability

It is certainly true that many people with dyslexia, for whom the development of literacy skills is difficult, have an aptitude for visual and spatial skills. However, this is not, as has sometimes been implied, an automatic consequence of being dyslexic. Those individuals fortunate enough to have a strong compensatory cognitive strength may well gravitate towards university courses in which this can be used to advantage, such as architecture, fine art and engineering. But the cognitive profile of people with dyslexia, while conforming to specific diagnostic criteria, may be as varied as that of the population as a whole.

Dyslexia as a continuum: the interaction of causes and effects

Depending on the nature of the core deficit, the efficacy of teaching intervention and the compensatory strengths of the individual, the effects of dyslexia may be mild, moderate or severe. In some cases, a relatively mild deficit may have severe effects and, conversely, some individuals with a severe phonological deficit may have developed such good compensatory strategies that the effects of dyslexia are significantly mitigated.

Many students come to university with a diagnosis of mild dyslexia. This usually means that there is little evidence of dyslexia in the student's levels of attainment in literacy skills.

However, if there is evidence of a cognitive weakness as described above, a diagnosis of dyslexia might still be appropriate. Such students might require less support than those whose literacy skills are more compromised by their specific learning difficulty. As in all conditions in which there is a continuum of severity, the question of where to draw the line in diagnosis is raised.

Where there is a family history of dyslexia, students who have not been assessed before coming to university may recognise that they share cognitive styles and some literacy problems with a relative who is dyslexic and may suspect that they are also dyslexic. While this may be the case, it is also possible to exhibit some features of a disorder without fulfilling all the diagnostic criteria – in such cases, a diagnosis of dyslexia would not be appropriate.

Late diagnosis

It is surprising how many students present for assessment for the first time when they come to university and who are subsequently identified as dyslexic. Such individuals may have attended school at a time when dyslexia was often overlooked; some may be extremely able and, having chosen their A-level subjects to reflect their strengths, may not have been substantially affected by their SpLD until they were required to write essays and to read vast amounts of text for their university course. There are few degree courses which do not place demands on students' literacy skills.

Other students may begin to wonder if they are dyslexic because they find the study skills required at university hard to master. If they have no history of difficulty in learning to read and write, the likelihood is that they are not dyslexic – it is quite normal to find the adjustment to university studies challenging, but this in itself does not indicate a SpLD.

Putting dyslexia in perspective

Coming to terms with a recent diagnosis of dyslexia, or even accommodating an early diagnosis as an adult, can be challenging at an emotional and psychological level. Many students will never before have received a diagnostic assessment report, and they may not know much about dyslexia, except insofar as it affects their own studies. It is perhaps useful to know that, as a SpLD, the core deficit in dyslexia is limited to a small number of cognitive processes which are in no way related to intelligence or other abilities. It is only because dyslexia affects literacy skills, which are so highly valued by so many societies worldwide, that the disorder has such a high profile. Many individuals have equivalent cognitive weaknesses in, for example, spatial awareness or musicality, but as the effects of such deficits are unlikely to affect their academic studies, they are unlikely to be considered to have a SpLD or cognitive disorder.

Other specific learning difficulties

Along with the ongoing research about dyslexia has come information about other SpLDs, some of which share aspects in common with dyslexia, or simply coexist with dyslexia.

Dyspraxia

Diagnostic assessments may reveal a pattern of strengths and weaknesses consistent with dyspraxia. Some reports may conclude that a particular individual is dyslexic but may also have elements of dyspraxia. Dyspraxia is a SpLD characterised primarily by difficulties with fine and gross motor coordination. The Dyspraxia Foundation offers the following definition:

> Developmental dyspraxia is an impairment or immaturity of the organisation of movement. It is an immaturity in the way that the brain processes information, which results in messages not being properly or fully transmitted. The term dyspraxia comes from the word praxis, which means 'doing, acting'. Dyspraxia affects the planning of what to do and how to do it. It is associated with problems of perception, language and thought.
>
> (<http://www.dyspraxiafoundation.org.uk>)

'Planning' refers to the neural programming of movement rather than to intentional preparation for movement, and the way in which dyspraxia might affect thought processes is little understood, but problems associated with speech (developmental verbal dyspraxia) have been researched (Stackhouse 1992).

Dyspraxic students may have organisational difficulties, poor handwriting, a poor sense of direction and difficulty with sports. Dyslexia and dyspraxia may coexist, and, therefore, it is most important to understand the areas of difficulty faced by a particular student. More information about dyspraxia can be found at <http://www.dyspraxiafoundation.org.uk>.

Attention Deficit Hyperactivity Disorder and Attention Deficit Disorder

Attention Deficit Hyperactivity Disorder (ADHD) and Attention Deficit Disorder (ADD) are SpLDs which have received increasing attention in recent years, particularly in children. In contrast to dyslexia and dyspraxia, which are usually diagnosed by either psychologists or specialist teachers, ADHD and ADD are generally diagnosed by medical doctors. The diagnosis is based on observed behaviours, which may include distractability, difficulty focusing on tasks, impulsivity and poor concentration. Individuals with ADHD or ADD are sometimes prescribed drugs which may help them to concentrate. Students with either of these disorders may find it difficult to sit through lectures or to apply themselves to long periods of study. The term ADD is more often applied to adults who may no longer demonstrate hyperactivity.

Scotopic Sensitivity Syndrome

Scotopic Sensitivity Syndrome (SSS), also known as Meares-Irlen Syndrome or Irlen Syndrome (Irlen 1991), refers to a visual processing disorder which is sometimes confused with dyslexia but often coexists with it. Although little is understood about the physiological basis for this disorder, there has been considerable research into effective treatment. People with SSS may find it difficult to discriminate between the foreground and the background in text. This results in visual discomfort, particularly when trying to read black print on a white background. Adults (and children) report symptoms of print 'moving' or 'dancing' on the page. They may see a page of print in a distorted way, sometimes with a 'river effect' in which the white background appears to travel through the print. Other reported distortions include a swirl effect and a double-image effect. It is not uncommon for people with SSS to find it difficult to read for long periods of time; indeed, the symptoms may not be present when they first begin to read but may appear after a period of time. The effects may also be worse when the individual is tired, under stress or reading with poor lighting.

Although a full optical assessment is recommended, people with SSS may have normal visual acuity, and opticians may not be able to offer an explanation for the reported symptoms. Moreover, even those individuals who require corrective lenses to address problems with visual acuity usually find that the processing difficulties persist. However, research conducted in the USA (Irlen 1983) and in the UK (Wilkins et al. 2004, Wilkins 2002, Evans 2001) has demonstrated that the effects of SSS can be minimised by placing coloured overlays over print or by using tinted spectacles. A colour which works for one person may not help someone else, so it is important for individuals to be assessed properly to determine what colour might be helpful.

Dyscalculia

The Department for Education and Skills (DfES, now DCSF) defines dyscalculia as

> a condition that affects the ability to acquire arithmetical skills. Dyscalculic learners may have difficulty understanding simple number concepts, lack an intuitive grasp of numbers and have problems learning number facts and procedures. Even if they produce a correct answer or use a correct method, they may do so mechanically and without confidence.

It goes on to say, 'purely dyscalculic learners who have difficulties only with number will have cognitive and language abilities in the normal range and may excel in non-mathematical subjects. It is more likely that difficulties with numeracy accompany the language difficulties of dyslexia' (DfES, now DCSF 1991).

Asperger Syndrome

Asperger Syndrome is a developmental disorder within the autism spectrum, characterised by problems with social interaction, communication, imagination and flexibility of thought. Problems encountered at university include difficulty collaborating with others in group-work sessions, difficulty relating to peers and difficulty adapting to changes in routine or lifestyle. Students with Asperger Syndrome may also have diagnoses of dyslexia, but their literacy difficulties and their problems with study usually differ from those typically encountered by dyslexic students. Students with Asperger Syndrome have difficulty generalising information, making inferences in oral and written communication, recognising the relevance of studying topics which do not interest them and prioritising study tasks. They may also have difficulty with time management and with the structuring of written assignments. As one of the diagnostic criteria for Asperger Syndrome is motor clumsiness (Gillberg 1991), students frequently have handwriting difficulties. For more information about Asperger Syndrome and its management at university, refer to Jamieson and Jamieson (2004).

> **Student tip:** *Make sure that you talk to someone in the dyslexia unit or the disability unit in your university to find out how you might be assessed for SpLDs or related problems which may affect your studies. You may find that simple adjustments can be made to help you gain the most from your course.*

Key points from Chapter 1

- Dyslexia is a cognitive disorder with a genetic basis.

- The core deficit in dyslexia is usually a weakness in processing speech sounds.

- The effects of dyslexia vary widely depending on a range of individual and environmental factors.

- Dyslexia is not related to intelligence.

- Many students are identified as dyslexic for the first time at university.

- Other specific learning difficulties, while independent of dyslexia (e.g. dyspraxia, ADHD/ADD, Scotopic Sensitivity Syndrome), may co-occur with dyslexia and may have additional effects on learning and literacy.

- The learning, study and literacy difficulties experienced by students with Asperger Syndrome are likely to differ from those experienced by students with dyslexia.

2

Assessment and Diagnosis of Dyslexia in Higher Education

AUDIENCE dyslexic students and their parents or family members, disability staff, academic staff

The DfES Report 2005

In 2003, the DfES, now DIUS convened a working party to develop guidance for the diagnostic assessment of SpLDs in Higher Education (HE). The group was formed in response to requests from local-authority awards officers who were finding it increasingly difficult to evaluate the evidence provided in reports supporting applications for the Disabled Students' Allowances (DSA). There was general consensus that reports lacked consistency in style, length and content.

As awards officers make decisions about individual students' eligibility for the DSA on the basis of the evidence in assessment reports, the process of assessment needed to be made more consistent, and acceptable standards needed to be established. It is hoped that, in the near future, in response to new advice on the content and format of diagnostic reports, local-authority officers will have confidence in the evidence they receive of students' SpLDs and that the evidence will be accessible and clearly set out in accordance with the agreed format. Whereas in the past, local-authority officers have often been unsure whether they should only accept reports written by psychologists, or whether those written by specialist teachers were also acceptable, the issue of assessors' qualifications has now also been addressed.

The working group report was published in July 2005 (see PATOSS and DfES, now DIUS websites). Guidelines cover diagnostic criteria, the aspects of performance and skills which should be assessed, suitable tests for use in diagnostic assessment, the assessment report format, the qualifications and certification of assessors and the training which assessors are required to undergo. The guidelines are summarised below.

The diagnostic criteria for dyslexia

A history of difficulty with the acquisition of literacy skills

Students are likely to have been late in learning to read, to have had difficulty reading aloud, to have been slow and inaccurate readers, to have been unsuccessful in learning to read and write through phonic teaching methods and to have a history of poor spelling.

Difficulties may not have been formally identified or even acknowledged by teachers and family. Conversely, students may not remember having problems but may have been told by others that they did indeed experience them. Some students may also have experienced problems in the development of speech and language. The vast majority will have had difficulty learning second languages at school. In some, but not all cases, arithmetic computation skills may be very weak.

Persisting difficulty with literacy skills

Although the effects of dyslexia change over time, they are always evident and can be identified through assessment. Even students who have developed good literacy skills through effective teaching and compensatory strengths demonstrate differences in the way they process text, both for reading and writing. Likely areas of weakness or difference are outlined in Chapter 5.

Evidence of a cognitive deficit in phonological processing

A history of difficulty acquiring literacy skills and persisting problems could be attributable to a variety of causes such as lack of educational opportunity. However, the diagnosis of SpLD requires evidence of an underlying weakness in certain aspects of cognitive processing. Weaknesses are likely to be found in the area of processing speech sounds (phonological processing) and auditory working memory. Students may also have problems with visual memory or with the integration of fine motor skills and visual processes.

Exclusion of other factors

It is important to consider other possible barriers to learning including sensory impairment, English as a second or additional language, educational experience and limited opportunities for learning, other SpLDs such as dyspraxia and ADHD and pervasive developmental disorders such as Asperger Syndrome. In some cases, persisting literacy difficulties may be entirely attributable to one or more of these factors, in which case a diagnosis of dyslexia would not be appropriate. Alternatively, one or more of these other barriers to learning may co-occur with dyslexia. It is the role of the assessor to attempt to tease apart possible causes of persisting literacy difficulties.

IQ/attainment discrepancy

In line with a large body of research in the field of dyslexia (Frederickson and Reason 1995, Howe 1997, Miles 1996, Siegel 1999, Stanovich and Stanovich 1997), diagnosis of dyslexia is not based on the identification of a discrepancy between underlying ability and literacy levels but on the criteria outlined above. It is expected that in most cases university students will demonstrate such a discrepancy in the assessment. However, this discrepancy is not a diagnostic criterion.

Some students with a moderate or below-average IQ have a deficit in phonological processing skills and fulfill all the diagnostic criteria for dyslexia. For such students, a diagnosis of dyslexia is considered appropriate. While a significant discrepancy between ability and achievement often gives rise to concern that a student might be dyslexic, and provides supporting evidence for diagnosis, there is no theoretical reason why less able students should not also be dyslexic.

As information about the broader aspects of students' cognitive skills is relevant to subsequent teaching intervention and to the ways in which students will develop compensatory strategies, the assessment of underlying ability is an important component of assessment. The assessment of verbal and non-verbal ability allows the effects of the SpLD to be considered within the broader context of the student's strengths and relative weaknesses.

Students with English as a second or additional language

The DfES report acknowledges that the assessment of students for whom English is a second or additional language (ESOL) presents assessors with particular challenges. Standardised tests have, for the most part, been developed on English-speaking populations, and the teasing apart of language difficulties and SPLDs involves particular skill on the part of the assessor. It is recommended that assessment of ESOL students should be carried out by assessors with appropriate experience in this area, although, when possible, an assessment in the student's mother tongue might be preferable.

Appropriately experienced assessors will apply their knowledge of the student's dominant language in establishing the extent to which English as an additional language (EAL) issues are affecting literacy skills. It is often reasonably easy to establish that EAL students are not dyslexic. For example, they may not have a history of difficulty acquiring literacy skills in their own (alphabetic) language; they may demonstrate very good decoding skills; they may also demonstrate good phonological skills, and their pattern of errors in reading and writing may clearly relate to the differences between their dominant language and English. It is much more difficult to make a positive diagnosis, but this would be indicated if the student appeared to meet the diagnostic criteria of a history of literacy difficulties, showed particular patterns of error (e.g., in spelling) and weakness in the cognitive skills known to underlie dyslexia. It is often possible to devise informal spoonerism tests (the transposition of initial sounds in a pair of words) in the student's first language and, depending on the word length of letters and digits, to test letter-naming and digit-naming in the first language. When such adaptations are made to test administration, standardised scores should, of course, *not* be quoted in the report, but a qualitative description of performance should be given. Specific ideas, such as this, are not given in the DfES report.

When is a reassessment necessary?

Assessments which have been carried out after the age of sixteen are considered appropriate for DSA eligibility. The DfES, now DIUS guidance states that students who were last assessed prior to the age of sixteen or who were assessed more than ten years previously require an 'Assessment of Performance Attainment' or top-up assessment which would provide an update on their current performance in reading, writing and spelling, which is likely to have changed significantly since the last assessment. Underlying ability, or intelligence, is likely to remain more stable, so there is no requirement for another assessment of intelligence. 'The top up diagnosis is to establish the likely impact of the student's specific learning difficulties on the skills needed for higher education' (<http://www.dfes.gov.uk/studentsupport/administrators/doc/DSA%guidance.doc>).

A reassessment may also be indicated if the evidence of dyslexia provided in previous reports is insufficient. For example, reports produced for the purpose of requesting access arrangements for GCSE and A-level examinations are not focused on diagnosis and are therefore not acceptable as evidence to support an application for DSA. Students whose only assessment has been of this type will need a full diagnostic assessment.

What should be assessed?

In order to establish whether a student is dyslexic according to the criteria outlined above, it is necessary to assess literacy skills, phonological processing skills and other aspects of cognitive functioning such as short-term memory. Additionally, of course, a detailed history should be taken to elicit relevant information about the development of any difficulties. An assessment of underlying ability, in the form of an IQ test giving measures of both verbal and non-verbal ability, should also be included unless previously assessed and reported.

Which tests should be used?

Tests should be selected to cover the full range of skills and abilities needed to identify the presence of dyslexia. Some tests will be standardised so that results can be considered in relation to the performance of others of the same age. It is therefore important that tests have been standardised on an adult population. It is not appropriate to use tests that give, for example, a reading or spelling age when assessing adults whose actual age is above the ceiling of the test. In addition to standardised tests, assessors may gather qualitative data using other materials. The results obtained from assessment procedures should yield both quantitative and qualitative data for interpretation. Some of the recommended tests are 'closed', that is, they can be used only by psychologists. Others are 'open' so can be used by specialist teachers. Recommended tests are listed in the final report of the DfES working party and are listed on the DfES, now DIUS website, grouped according to the skills concerned (e.g., reading, spelling, cognitive processing). An ongoing committee has been formed since publication of the 2005 DfES report to monitor and update the list on a regular basis.

The assessment process

Students who have not previously been assessed and are referred for diagnostic assessment are frequently unaware of what to expect. They may have just popped in to the office of the dyslexia coordinator during a break between classes hoping for a quick 'test' to see if they are dyslexic. They are surprised when they learn that a full diagnostic assessment may take up to four hours, although it is usually completed in less time.

Screening

Because the assessment procedure is highly specialised and time-intensive, as well as being expensive, many universities have some form of screening to determine which students should be put forward for a full assessment. The screening usually consists of a structured interview to identify if there are other probable causes for difficulties the student is encountering. Students may be requested to bring in a piece of free writing and may also be asked to complete tasks designed to identify if there is evidence of a weak short-term memory or an underlying phonological deficit. In some cases, screening may take the form of a short computerised assessment. A questionnaire, or structured interview form, for use in screening or assessment is included in the resources section and on the CD.

Full assessment

When someone is referred for a full diagnostic assessment, the assessor will take into account the information from the screening and then administer a range of other tests. These will include standardised tests which highlight difficulties with reading, writing and spelling, as well as assessments which provide evidence of difficulties with visual and phonological processing. Most assessments will also include a battery of non-literacy-based tasks to determine the individual's underlying ability.

The recommended format for a diagnostic assessment report

The DfES report provides detailed guidance, including a pro forma, for the presentation of diagnostic assessment reports. A greater level of consistency among assessors should facilitate the perusal of reports by local-authority officers and others who need to make decisions about DSA eligibility.

Assessment reports should reflect the diagnostic criteria outlined above. The main sections of the report should be:

- **Background information:** A summary of the student's developmental, educational and family history, including language background, previous assessments and previous support and access arrangements.
- **Attainments in literacy:** Performance in reading prose and single words, spelling and writing.
- **Underlying ability:** Verbal and non-verbal skills (which may include tests of working memory).
- **Cognitive processing:** Performance in tests of processes known to underlie dyslexia, e.g., phonological processing, working memory, visual processing speed, etc.
- **Conclusion:** Drawing together of the evidence with a statement as to whether a diagnosis of dyslexia is indicated.
- **Recommended support:** A brief statement about the type of support from which the student would be likely to benefit. Recommendations should not be too detailed, as the student will need to have an Assessment of Need for DSA purposes, and individual universities will have their own systems in place for supporting students with dyslexia. However, it is useful if the assessor states whether adjustment, such as extra time in exams, would be appropriate.

In addition to these main sections, there should be a cover sheet with the student's personal details (date of birth, university, course, etc.) and details of the assessor, including the issuing body and number of their practising certificate. There should also be a summary page, placed immediately after the cover sheet, outlining the diagnosis, evidence and effects on study and literacy skills. Appendices should include a summary of scores and a short description of tests administered.

Who is qualified to administer assessments?

Psychologists and specialist teachers who are Associate Members of the British Dyslexia Association (AMBDA) or those who are eligible for membership are qualified to administer diagnostic assessments. From September 2007, specialist teachers need to have a practising certificate issued by an approved professional body. Currently, practising certificates are awarded by the Professional Association of Teachers of Students with Specific Learning Difficulties (PATOSS) and Dyslexia Action (formerly the Dyslexia Institute).

Routes to qualification

Route 1

Specialist teachers eligible for associate membership of the BDA will automatically be awarded a practising certificate if they apply to PATOSS or Dyslexia Action (see websites). Applicants who are not already members of the professional body to which they apply need to become members before a certificate is awarded, in order to ensure that they undertake to abide by the relevant code of ethics. Certificates are valid for three years, after which evidence of Continuing Professional Development (CPD) will be requested before a replacement certificate is issued.

Route 2

Specialist teachers who do not hold one of the approved qualifications leading to eligibility for AMBDA may apply for practising certificates through accreditation of prior learning (APL) and/or accreditation of prior experience (APE). A portfolio must be submitted with evidence of training, qualifications and experience, including video recordings of the administration of diagnostic assessments and their respective reports.

Route 3

Specialist teachers who have no training in diagnostic assessment (including the use of psychometric tests) need to seek further training, the details of which are specified in the DfES, now DIUS, report.

Route 4

Applicants who have no SpLD specialist training need to seek training that will provide qualifications at AMBDA level (NVQ Level 7) or equivalent.

The National Committee for Standards in Assessment, Training and Practice (informally known as SASC: SpLD Assessment Standards Committee)

In order to monitor the implementation of the DfES, now DIUS, guidance for assessment, a national committee was formed at the behest of the DfES, now DIUS, following on from the publication of the 2005 working-group report. Professional bodies represented on the committee include the Association of Dyslexia Specialists in Higher Education (ADSHE), Dyslexia Action (DA), the British Dyslexia Association (BDA), The Professional Association of Teachers of Students with Specific Learning Difficulties (PATOSS) the British Psychological Society (BPS), the London Language and Literacy Unit (LLLU+) and the Helen Arkell Dyslexia Centre (HADC). The remit of SASC is to approve training courses in assessment, successful completion of which would lead to eligibility for practising certificates, to develop guidelines for CPD, and to establish the criteria for institutions wishing to award practising certificates. SASC meets three times a year and is currently chaired by the Chief Executive of PATOSS. Minutes of meetings and other documents can be found on the PATOSS website (<http://www.patoss-dyslexia.org>).

Funding and procedures for assessment

DSA assessments of need (Chapter 4) are funded through the DSA, but there is no DSA funding for diagnostic assessments. Students who are eligible (i.e., home students who are applying for the full student loan) may claim funding for assessment through the Access to Learning Fund (ALF) administered by their universities. However, this funding is awarded at the discretion of individual universities, so students should not assume that they will receive reimbursement. In some cases, institutions may decide to fund part of the cost. Sample application forms for ALF are included in the Resources section.

Some universities provide assessments on site, either through their own specialist dyslexia staff or through assessors employed on a freelance basis. Other universities may be able to recommend assessors for students who have not been assessed before and for those needing top-up assessments. As the procedures and administrative structures of institutions vary widely, students should approach their dyslexia-support service for advice about how to go about arranging an assessment.

The assessment report

Within two to three weeks after the diagnostic assessment, students should receive their confidential diagnostic assessment report. In some universities, the assessor may have a meeting with the student within a few weeks of the assessment to provide feedback on the report. If students do not have the opportunity to discuss their report with the assessor, they may be able to arrange feedback with the university's specialist dyslexia or disability staff.

Although it is necessary for the student to send a copy of the report to DSA award officers as evidence of dyslexia, copies of the report will not generally be sent by the assessor to anyone other than the student and certainly not without their permission – it will be up to the student to make copies as appropriate.

The report should be written in accessible style with scores and interpretations clearly explained. If this is not the case, students may need to discuss their report with the university's disability or specialist dyslexia staff.

Response to diagnosis

On an emotional level, a mature adult who left school with few, if any, qualifications may experience a range of reactions to gaining a place at university. Often such students have low self-esteem resulting from years of perceived failure (see Chapter 3, Morgan and Klein 2000). In fact, the 'failure' may not have been theirs but rather a school system that was unable to identify the reasons why a particular child did not seem to learn in the expected manner. However, as the onus for poor performance was placed on the individual student, the sense of failure is often internalised and is very difficult to shed. Moreover, when individuals are first diagnosed as dyslexic in their late twenties, thirties or even older, a common response is relief accompanied with anger.

> 'My first feelings when I learned I was dyslexic were those of relief and anger – relief that I could give up the stigma I had carried for so many years – the words of my teachers saying, 'try harder' and 'don't be so lazy'. But then there was a surge of anger – I did not want to be dyslexic. Being a mature student with no formal qualifications hindered me enough, but now I had an added disadvantage.'

Anger may be directed at parents, former teachers and/or the school system. The newly discovered explanation for their many years of struggle may allow students to cast off previous labels such as 'thick', 'lazy' and 'stupid' which may have been with them since childhood. However, the new label of 'dyslexia' is one that might require time and considerable explanation to understand. Some people are resistant to the concept of labels, making it essential for the diagnostic assessor to offer a careful and accessible explanation of the individual's profile.

Benefits of assessment to previously undiagnosed students

Many adults who enter university with a history of academic struggle are concerned when they realise that the same problems that confronted them when they were at school resurface during their university course. In fact, even those students who have managed to develop good coping strategies may find that these are no longer adequate when faced with the increasing academic demands placed on them by university courses. They may find it difficult to keep up with the reading load, meet deadlines for coursework submission, take effective notes in lectures or succeed in examinations. There are several benefits of diagnosis for students in this situation:

- For the first time, they will be able to understand why they struggle with academic work.
- A diagnosis of dyslexia may replace labels such as 'thick', 'lazy' or 'stupid' which had been assigned to them in the past.
- Once they have a formal assessment outlining the nature of their strengths and weaknesses, they will be able to address their learning by developing their strengths to overcome their weaknesses.
- Home students who have a diagnosis will be able to access funding through the DSA to provide assistive technology and relevant learning support.

The benefits of assessment will, in most instances, outweigh the emotional effects of late diagnosis and should provide a basis for a positive approach to the challenges posed by HE.

> 'Looking back, it is all too easy to remember the educational equivalents of public humiliation or tar and feathering... far from forgiving my tormenters today I would not pass up the opportunity to get even – yes, it hurts that bad. I remember (after diagnosis) a tremendous tidal wave of relief, overwhelming, drowning relief. I was not 'stupid', 'dumb', 'slow', 'lazy', 'hopeless', 'backward'. I was dyslexic and I could do something about it. The effects? Coupled with the emotions came the dubious prospect of shedding tears in public.'

> 'I am not afraid of being dyslexic, but I'm afraid of not being [dyslexic] since that would mean I have an even greater problem. Becoming a full-time degree student was such a significant step in my life. But at the moment, I can't enjoy the course because my mind is clouded with so much self-doubt – I need to be free of this.'

Key points from Chapter 2

- The DfES working group report (2005) contains guidance covering assessment of SpLDs in HE.

- The diagnostic criteria for SpLDs specified in the report are: a history of difficulty acquiring literacy skills, persisting difficulty and an underlying weakness in particular areas of cognitive functioning.

- Assessments less than ten years old and conducted after the age of sixteen are accepted as evidence of SpLD for DSA application purposes.

- When IQ has been assessed and reported previously, it does not need to be reassessed if the student is able to produce a copy of the report.

- Students at university who have never been previously assessed may be able to arrange a screening to determine whether a full diagnostic assessment is indicated.

- Reports should contain background information, details of attainment in literacy skills and details of cognitive functioning. Tests used should be appropriate for adults and should be interpreted both qualitatively and quantitatively.

- From September 2007, specialist teacher assessors will need practising certificates.

- Diagnostic assessments are not funded through the DSA, but eligible students may apply to the ALF.

- The benefits of a first diagnosis at university in terms of gaining insight into the cause of problems and in terms of support available often outweigh any apparent disadvantage.

3

Dyslexic Students in Higher Education

AUDIENCE   dyslexic students and academic staff

The dyslexic students who are likely to progress to courses in HE include two broad groups: namely, those who were diagnosed at school and may or may not have received specialist teaching, and those who are assessed after they begin their course in HE. The response to their difficulties with academic pursuits may correlate with the age (and stage of education) at which they were assessed as well as the interventions that were (or were not) implemented.

Students with an existing diagnosis

Students who already know that they are dyslexic before entering university are often at an advantage over those who have never benefited from a full assessment. As dyslexic profiles differ from one person to the next, it is difficult to make generalisations, but, nonetheless, there are some patterns which are likely to emerge. The following discussion assumes some general similarities among students who have shared common experiences, but obviously will not apply equally to all individuals.

Until the late 1980s, children who exhibited problems with learning to read and write at primary school were sometimes considered lazy or even not very 'intelligent'. However, as a result of the introduction of the first Special Educational Needs (SEN) Code of Practice in 1994 (<http://www.dfes.gov.uk/publications/guidanceonthelaw/dfeepub>), a staged framework was put in place whereby children who were not acquiring basic skills could be formally monitored within the school, with outside agencies, including educational psychologists, becoming involved at the later stages. The Code of Practice has been revised since to take account of the Disability Discrimination Act (DDA) (1995) and SENDA (2001) (see Chapter 4).

As awareness of dyslexia became more widespread during the 1990s, some teachers and parents began to associate certain learning behaviours with the possibility that the child was dyslexic, and arrangements were sometimes made for full diagnostic assessments. Local authorities employed educational psychologists to administer in-depth testing to arrive at a better understanding of the child's cognitive profile, but many local authorities would not agree to assessment unless a child's levels of attainment were in the bottom 2 per cent. These pupils were the only ones who were given SEN statements. Those children who were fortunate enough to have their learning difficulties identified may have received extra tuition in an attempt to help them overcome their problems with reading, writing and spelling. As these students progressed through the system, they most likely benefited from special examination arrangements for GCSEs and A-levels and were therefore more apt to gain results that reflected their true abilities. Many of those who achieved the required grades were offered places at university, where they might have been granted similar examination arrangements (usually extra time and possibly sympathetic consideration for spelling and written expression). Indeed, in the early 1990s, some of these students were able to apply for the newly instituted DSAs and might have been able to purchase a computer with a spell-check. However, the number of identified dyslexic students entering HE at that time was relatively small.

The changing profile of students in HE

There has been a continual rise in the number of students with SpLDs entering university during the past ten to fifteen years. This can be attributed largely to two factors. First, the fact that more children are assessed and supported through school has led to an increase in the number of students who succeed in A-levels and gain acceptance to HE. These students usually have an awareness of their learning styles and tend to be proactive in ensuring that they apply for the support available at university.

Second, there has been a concerted effort by universities to increase the number of students with disabilities who gain admission to courses across the board. The Widening Participation agenda in HE, coupled with legal obligations to provide support for students with SpLDs and other disabilities have both had an impact on student recruitment. The under-representation of students with disabilities in HE in the early 1990s was recognised by the Government who targeted this group for recruitment as part of Widening Participation. Indeed, the Higher Education Funding Council for England (HEFCE) allocated funds for projects specifically designed to identify the needs of these students and to develop appropriate support systems. For the first time, universities were actively encouraged to include students with disabilities in their admission targets. Because dyslexic students form the largest group of disabled students, many projects have been funded to address the ways in which institutions can accommodate their needs.

The twenty-first century has seen major changes in the composition of student bodies at British universities. In addition to an increase in the number of students with declared disabilities (including those who arrive at university with a diagnosis of dyslexia), the number of mature students has also risen dramatically. Many adults who did not have conventional qualifications such as A-levels have re-entered education and gained equivalent qualifications through other routes, such as NVQs or access courses. As the Government has set the target of increasing university attendance to 50 per cent of school leavers, the profile of the student population in HE will undoubtedly continue to change. As more and more 'non-traditional' students apply to university and as the range of degree courses develops, students who were previously denied entry to university are now being offered a 'second chance'. Many of these students may be able people with dyslexia, who were never identified as having a SpLD at school and who now bring the benefit of maturity and experience to their studies. However, the problems they had at school are likely to resurface and, as a result of increased awareness and knowledge, they may put themselves forward for a diagnostic assessment.

Widening Participation efforts included attempts to attract students from diverse cultural and socio-economic backgrounds not typically represented in HE prior to the 1990s. Financial incentives have encouraged institutions to set up alternative routes for admission to HE, and a close liaison has been forged with Further Education colleges who developed access courses for mature students.

Mature students

The proliferation of access courses provided opportunities for many mature students to gain university acceptance. While it is recognised that mature students bring with them a wealth of life experience and related skills, they may also be those students who did not succeed at school and therefore had not applied to university through the traditional routes. Many of these students are dyslexic, but they were not identified as such while at school. For these students, admission to and success at university may involve a complex set of adjustments, both emotional and academic.

As the changing trend in education brings in more and more students who do not conform to the traditional entry routes, the student body at many institutions has become far more varied, posing new challenges to those who teach in HE. The increasingly diverse student population includes students who are speakers of other languages, who may not be fluent in English. Additionally, students may represent a wide age range, rather than being focused primarily on eighteen-year-old entrants. Students who are newcomers to Britain enrich the cultural diversity of the student body. There may, of course, be dyslexic students among these differing student groups. And, finally, the changes in legislation have resulted in opening doors to students with a range of disabilities who previously would have been denied access to university. Dyslexic students, as well as those with other SpLDs, have always been under-represented in HE, but their increasing number has created a challenge necessitating a rethinking of pedagogic approaches, both in terms of teaching methods as well as in how to assess the attainment of course outcomes.

Choice of degree subject

One advantage of a full diagnostic assessment is that it provides an understanding of an individual's cognitive strengths and weaknesses. Following diagnosis, a student may feel a sense of relief when finally given an explanation for earlier difficulties with literacy-based tasks. However, the profile of strengths and weaknesses may also impact on choice of degree. Although being dyslexic does not in itself dictate a person's chances of success in a particular area, it is important for students to look at their own strengths and weaknesses alongside the demands of their chosen field. For example, someone who has major difficulties with reading, writing and spelling in English might find it difficult to pursue a degree in journalism. However, it may be that the reverse is true – many dyslexic journalism students who have problems with proofreading and attending to detail, such as crossing 't's and dotting 'i's, may still be excellent reporters or feature-story writers. Indeed, once in employment, they have the benefit of copy-editors to attend to the finer transcriptional aspects of writing. Career choice should be influenced by a careful weighing of the required employment skills and an individual's strengths and weaknesses. Ultimately, the decision to pursue a particular course of study should depend on how successful students' coping strategies are in overcoming the effects of their dyslexia. This may also be influenced by the ability of course tutors to adapt their teaching and assessment methods to account for possible variations in student profiles.

> *Student Tip:* Before deciding on what course of study to pursue, find out about the course requirements and skills necessary for potential future careers. Then examine your own strengths and weaknesses. This will help you determine whether you can devise strategies to overcome any possible obstacles to success.

Varying demands on literacy skills

Although academic success conventionally depends on competence in literacy, there are many subjects in which students can use other cognitive and personal strengths to great advantage. Some have excellent visuo-spatial skills and an aptitude for three-dimensional thinking. Such students often choose to study subjects such as design, architecture or engineering. Many creative dyslexic students gravitate towards fine art, a subject in which there is less focus on essay-writing. Other students with dyslexia have very good reasoning abilities and are able to conceptualise complex information; they may be excellent mathematicians or physicists, also subjects in which there is less emphasis on writing.

Some students may also have high levels of compassion and empathy and may gravitate naturally to professions such as social work, nursing, radiography or teaching. There is no inherent reason why dyslexic students should not succeed in any academic discipline or profession, including law, medicine and other health-related fields. Indeed, there are many dyslexic people who have become renowned in their particular field, serving as good role models for occupations and professions across the board.

However, some courses, e.g. nursing, art and acting, which used to be based on practical training, have now become degree courses with an emphasis on academic attainment requiring large amounts of course work as well as exams. Such courses might unintentionally discriminate against potentially talented practitioners who find it difficult to show what they know on paper. Course leaders, in liaison with professional bodies, need to look carefully at the skills and knowledge required of their profession to determine whether students can demonstrate their knowledge through alternative forms of assessment.

Teaching and learning at university

Students entering university following completion of A levels or access courses are often poorly prepared for the demands placed on them by degree-level work. They may be accustomed to tutors providing very structured guidance on exactly what to read and what to include in assignments. The lack of specific instructions on what to do between lectures coupled with being expected to hand in many assignments for different modules at virtually the same time can come as quite a shock. Moreover, many students entering university from school or college are surprised at how little contact time they have with lecturers and tutors.

In contrast to the students' expectations, there is an assumption by academic lecturers that university students already have the requisite academic skills to produce coursework and pass exams. Therefore, there may be little explicit teaching of expected and necessary academic skills such as referencing, essay-writing, use of quotations, research skills and reading for academic purposes. The mismatch between the expectations of students and those of their lecturers can create a rocky start on the road to academic success for many students. Dyslexic students may find it particularly difficult to develop the necessary skills unless they receive explicit help. Some universities offer special bridging courses for dyslexic students to familiarise them with the expectations of higher education prior to beginning their courses.

> **Student Tip:** *Investigate whether your chosen university has study-skills modules or any provision such as bridging courses to encourage a smooth transition from school or college to university.*

Academic assessment at university

The balance between closed-book examinations and coursework seems to be in a constant state of flux. Until the 1970s, most degree courses were assessed solely through examinations. Gradually, coursework assumed greater importance until, in some cases, degrees were awarded almost entirely on the basis of assignments completed in the students' own time. The balance is now shifting again, largely because of concerns of academics about plagiarism and material lifted from the Internet. Some courses have 'take-home' examinations, in which students are given between twenty-four hours and a week to complete a piece of work with access to books, journals and the Internet.

Dyslexic students nearly all say that they work more slowly than their peers; they spend very much longer researching and writing coursework assignments, and they are very aware of the pressure of time in examinations. Generally, they accept this quite philosophically. The provision of extra time for closed-book examinations is therefore justified, and, whereas it is unlikely to be in students' best interests to be granted automatic extensions for coursework, tutors should generally be prepared to use their discretion if extra time is requested. For open-book or take-home examinations, it is reasonable to allow the same percentage of extra time as is granted for closed-book examinations.

Marking the work of dyslexic students

In order to be sure that dyslexic students are not treated unfairly, it is important to establish exactly what is being assessed in a piece of coursework or in an examination. Clear marking criteria not only lead to greater consistency between markers, but they involve making explicit decisions about whether, for example, students need to demonstrate good spelling ability or whether punctuation is one of the competences being assessed (see Chapter 6 for a full explanation of 'competence standards'). In many cases, spelling is not included as a specific marking criterion. Therefore, marks should not be deducted for spelling errors, whether the student is dyslexic or not. The same would apply to minor inaccuracies and errors in punctuation or omissions of word endings frequently made by dyslexic students. There should be no need to differentiate between the scripts of dyslexic and non-dyslexic students on the basis of these features of their writing if they are not explicitly being assessed.

In subjects such as English or foreign languages, in which correct spelling is deemed important, the number of marks that can be lost for poor spelling should be stipulated. Usually only a small percentage (2–5 per cent) of marks is likely to be assigned specifically to spelling. It may be, therefore, that students with dyslexia will lose a small percentage of marks because of their weak spelling; but if spelling is important in their particular discipline, they have to accept this. In some cases, an apparently minor spelling error can lead to serious misinformation. For example, one letter creates a major difference in meaning between *dysphasia* (loss of language function) and *dysphagia* (swallowing difficulties). Dyslexic students will need to master distinctions such as this when they occur. Likewise, students studying computer programming will lose marks if they write the wrong code, since writing the correct code is an essential learning outcome or 'competence standard'.

Academic tutors should make students aware of the assessment criteria for their course modules. Although criteria will generally focus on content over form, the structure, coherence and cohesion of dyslexic students' written work cannot be overlooked if this interferes with the demonstration of their knowledge. Feedback should be constructive and selective (see Chapter 5 for a more detailed discussion).

The Association of Dyslexia Specialists in Higher Education (ADSHE)

One result of the implementation of the SENDA in 2002 was the fact that all universities became aware of the need to provide some designated support for students with disabilities, including SpLDs. As dyslexia is the most commonly reported disability in all Higher Education Statistics Agency (HESA) returns, most institutions have set up some form of dyslexia-specific provision. There continues to be quite a variation in the institutional location of the dyslexia support unit as well as the degree of staffing. However, a positive outcome has been that dyslexic students know that they can expect to find some provision for dyslexia support in any institution they choose and can therefore base their choice on the courses offered rather than on the support available.

In response to the increased number of jobs for dyslexia specialists, there emerged a desire to avoid 'reinventing the wheel'. As dyslexia provision often consists of one person shouldering the major responsibilities for dyslexia awareness for staff and support for students, a group of dyslexia coordinators and specialist tutors was convened in London in 2001 (Morgan 2005). The primary aim of this group was to share concerns and experiences and to overcome the sense of isolation which many practitioners faced in HE. Out of this meeting grew an association of dyslexia specialists across the UK who officially launched the Association of Dyslexia Specialists in HE (ADSHE) at the BDA International conference in March 2004. The stated objectives of ADSHE are:

- to act as a forum for discussion of the professional interests of dyslexia specialists in HE and to represent the professional and related interests of ADSHE members;
- to share knowledge and disseminate good practice, including promoting and developing the understanding of all aspects of dyslexia;
- to clarify and promote students' entitlement to dyslexia support within individual institutions and throughout the sector;
- to promote understanding of disability legislation in relation to students with dyslexia;
- to provide a professional viewpoint to relevant bodies such as the DfES, now DIUS and HEFCE on matters relating to HE students with dyslexia.

ADSHE's membership has grown dramatically since its inception in 2001. It now has more than 200 members representing ninety-nine institutions of HE (including some Further Education colleges that offer HE courses) in England, Wales, Scotland and Northern Ireland. Several regional subgroups have been established, and there is a yearly networking event attended by members from across the UK. In addition, members have access to a dedicated on-line discussion group so that collegial debate and discussion is available whenever members wish to raise issues relating to the implementation of new practice in their respective institutions.

ADSHE has provided a climate that allows dyslexia support services across the HE spectrum to develop their services to ensure that the experience of dyslexic students will be similar regardless of which institution they attend. This has been an important step towards standardising the support available to students, thus freeing them to select a course or university based on interest rather than on available support (<http://www.adshe.org.uk>).

Key points from Chapter 3

- Increasing numbers of students who have already been identified as dyslexic are now entering university.

- One result of Widening Participation initiatives is that students whose dyslexia was not identified at school are entering university through alternative academic routes.

- There is no reason why dyslexic students should not succeed in any academic discipline, depending on their individual strengths and aptitudes.

- Some degree subjects place greater demands on literacy skills than others, so it is worth making enquiries about the form coursework will take before applying.

- To ensure that the work of dyslexic students is marked fairly, assessment criteria should be specified in detail, on the basis of justifiable competence criteria.

- The maintenance of academic standards is not compromised within disability legislation.

- ADSHE is a forum through which dyslexia specialists based in universities can share information and develop guidance for good practice.

4

Dyslexia within the Disability Framework

AUDIENCE dyslexic students, disability/dyslexia staff, academic staff

The Disability Discrimination Act (1995) (DDA)

Setting the context

Although dyslexia was first identified over 100 years ago, the concept of dyslexic learning styles, identifying patterns of strengths and weaknesses has been recognised only relatively recently. Traditionally, dyslexic people did not succeed in education and were directed to more vocational, less academic courses. They trained to become car mechanics, chefs, hairdressers, welders, builders and other occupations that emphasised manual, rather than academic skills. In Britain, the 11+ examination was a selection mechanism which, because it was entirely based on written assessment, may have deprived many bright (unidentified) dyslexic children from pursuing an academic career. Prior to the establishment of comprehensive education in 1955, students who failed the 11+ examinations were allocated to secondary modern schools and were placed on a firm path leading towards non-professional, non-academic careers. Comprehensive education at least had the effect of picking up 'late bloomers' as well as those students who might have failed the 11+ but were nonetheless academically talented.

However, despite the post-war history of British education, the formal identification of dyslexic children did not take place with any regularity until about the 1990s. The first government Special Educational Needs (SEN) Code of Practice (1994) required schools to identify children with a range of special educational needs and to ensure that these needs were met through appropriate teaching and other intervention. For some children, this might have involved attendance at special schools, such as schools for the physically disabled or for visually or hearing-impaired children. For others, support was provided through special units within mainstream schools.

Unfortunately, however, dyslexic children often fell through the net, as the hidden nature of their difficulties, coupled with the expense of providing a diagnostic report, made it easy to overlook their needs. Moreover, teachers emerging from teacher-training courses often had little or no training in SpLDs and therefore did not pick up on the children in their classes who presented with learning difficulties. Even more damaging was the lack of understanding of bright children who may have eagerly contributed to class discussions but produced very poor written work. Teachers who were untrained to spot signs of SpLDs were suspicious when confronted with the discrepancy in what they expected from a child compared to the level of work submitted. They often attributed the poor level of written work to laziness and would report to parents that their child just 'needed to try harder'. The effect of this omission in training and the resultant lack of knowledge and understanding on the part of many teachers was that dyslexic children either lost interest in school or felt confused as to why they could not produce what was expected of them. An additional consequence was poor self-esteem, which, in turn, escalated into bad behaviour and, in some cases, caused truanting from school and anti-social or criminal activities (Morgan 1997).

Concurrent with government recognition of the existence of SpLDs, major lobbying took place by the BDA and the DA (formerly the Dyslexia Institute) to put pressure on schools to recognise and provide appropriate intervention for dyslexic children. Literacy campaigns in the 1980s contributed to the realisation that dyslexic children grew up to become dyslexic adults; the growing number of illiterate adults was a shocking statistic at that time. The implications for the fate of future generations became a major concern.

By the early 1990s, the Government's concern about the overall level of educational achievement heightened. In response to the problems inherent in producing a generation of children lacking formal qualifications, the Higher Education Funding Council in England (HEFCE) established funding for proposals aimed at widening participation. The funding allocation in 1993 was targeted at projects designed to recruit and support students with disabilities. The most successful proposals were those aimed at improving the support for dyslexic students. Since that time, there has been a burgeoning in numbers of dyslexic students gaining admission to universities, as well as those who are assessed and identified post-admission.

The Act

In 1995 the DDA established the principle that it is illegal to discriminate against anyone on the basis of a disability. This had far-reaching consequences in terms of opening doors for disabled people to participate in many areas of society which were previously unavailable to them. The Act became law in 2001 when the Special Educational Needs Disability Act (SENDA) came into force. According to SENDA (also known as Part IV of the DDA), institutions of further and higher education are obliged to provide for the needs of disabled students in all aspects of their education, from admission to completion of their course. One of the main precepts of this legislation is that institutions must provide 'reasonable adjustments' to accommodate disabled students. (See Chapter 6 for a discussion of what constitutes a reasonable adjustment.)

The Act further states that institutions have 'anticipatory duties' to put appropriate procedures in place to ensure that an individual is not placed at a 'substantial disadvantage'. It is unlawful to fail to make reasonable adjustments.

Under current disability legislation, dyslexia *may* be classed as a disability. Technically, this classification depends upon whether it can be shown that the nature of the 'disability' falls within the definition provided in the DDA. Under the Act, a person is considered disabled if he or she has a physical or mental impairment which has an effect on his or her ability to carry out normal day-to-day activities. The effect must be:

- substantial (that is, more than minor or trivial);
- adverse;
- long-term (that is, it has lasted or is likely to last for at least a year or for the rest of the life of the person affected).

To date, no case has been taken to court questioning whether an individual diagnostic report for dyslexia presents sufficient evidence to confirm that the individual is, in fact, 'disabled' under the law. Until such time as there is a court judgement to the contrary, it can be assumed that dyslexia is legally considered as a disability.

This legal underpinning laid the foundations for students with identified SpLDs to gain access to appropriate support. As the number of dyslexic students increased in HE, so too did the need to engage specialist support tutors to respond to the growing demand. Additional HEFCE grants over the years have funded projects designed to identify the needs of dyslexic students, to explore staff development and training issues and to establish specialist support units within universities. A survey carried out by the 1999 working party on Dyslexia in HE found that the incidence of dyslexia in HE was in the region of 1.2 per cent to 1.5 per cent, with 43 per cent of these being identified as dyslexic after admission (Singleton 1999).

The DDA and the SENDA were further modified by an Amendment (Further and Higher Education) Regulations 2006 which imposed duties on post-sixteen education providers as of September 2006. A Code of Practice prepared by the Disability Rights Commission (DRC) gives detailed guidance on the implementation of these duties and helps to clarify some of the ambiguities such as what is meant by a 'reasonable adjustment' under the law. (Further discussion of this is contained in Chapter 6.)

One of several changes to the DDA 1995 which took effect as of September 2006 is that the new Act states there are now four kinds of discrimination. These are: direct discrimination, failure to make reasonable adjustments, 'disability-related' discrimination and victimisation. Additionally, there are changes made in the scope of the Act which now incorporates specific provisions in relation to qualifications, prohibiting discriminatory advertisements, prohibiting instructions and pressure to discriminate, and specific duties that apply after a relationship has ended.

Additionally, the Disability Equality Duty (DED) required public authorities to be proactive in addressing disability equality issues and placed a duty on institutions to promote disability equality. Universities were required to publish disability equality schemes by December 2006 in which they demonstrate how they will fulfill both general and specific duties over a three-year period. After 2009, yearly progress reports need to be produced. The requirement to collect data on the performance and achievements of disabled students in HE (including academic performance, drop-out rates and successful transition to HE) should provide a much clearer picture of how well disabled students have been integrated into HE.

Dyslexia as a disability

The issue of disability raises questions on two counts. First, dyslexia exists on a continuum ranging from mild to severe difficulties. It is not unreasonable to query whether someone for whom the effects of dyslexia are minor can be classified as having a disability under the legislation. The important issue here is the determination of whether the difficulties that exist might impede the individual from attaining his or her full potential. If this can be shown to be true, it could be argued that the effects of the disability are 'substantial' under the law. There are, for example, able students who have developed extremely good coping strategies which serve to mask their difficulties. However, the time it takes to process information may disadvantage these individuals in a time-constrained examination. Moreover, in comparison to fellow students, it may require a great deal more time to complete the reading and coursework assignments. The result of these ongoing but not necessarily obvious problems may be that the student under-achieves. A student in this situation may be helped to achieve simply through the provision of a computer for coursework and extra time on exams.

Second, many dyslexic people do not see their learning difference as a disability. Often they have developed coping strategies which have enabled them to succeed either academically and/or professionally. Those who were diagnosed as children and received appropriate help at school may choose not to disclose their dyslexia at university. However, it is not uncommon for such students to approach the dyslexia service at their university at a later stage in their studies, when the effects of their dyslexia once again may become manifest in response to increased academic pressures. Indeed, some students come forward in the final year of their degrees, or even at postgraduate level, when they feel that their coping strategies are no longer adequate. Others may declare their dyslexia at the start of their course but simply want extra time on their examinations to ensure a level playing field and may choose not to have any further accommodations.

Other dyslexic students, often those who have been identified as dyslexic only after beginning university, want help to develop strategies to overcome obstacles to their success. These students may resist the label of 'disability' but, nonetheless, wish to avail themselves of the support provided through the DSA. It is important to have a discussion, preferably at the stage when they receive feedback regarding their diagnostic report, to encourage them to view the notion of disability within the defining legal characteristics so they can feel comfortable applying for the DSA.

The dyslexia 'label'

The location of the dyslexia support service within the institutional structure of the university may influence a student's decision about whether or not to take advantage of the available support. If the dyslexia support provision is located within disability services, some students may be reluctant to seek help because they don't perceive their difficulties as being a 'disability'. Indeed, dyslexia is often seen as a 'hidden disability' as there is no physical manifestation which can easily be identified. In fact, many bright dyslexic people manage to mask their symptoms through the use of well-practised adaptations. This may simply be the use of a spell-check on the computer or it may involve reliance on family or close friends to check over work, read texts aloud or even scribe coursework. The beginning of a degree course may be the first time that the student is separated from this support network, resulting in great anxiety in response to the challenge of developing new coping strategies and becoming an independent learner.

It is most important that support tutors as well as subject tutors, personal tutors, library staff and any other staff who work with dyslexic students are aware of the sensitivity caused by accepting a new 'label'. Likewise, students must be helped to feel comfortable with this label and should be offered regular specialist support to help them understand the nature of their particular dyslexic profile and to use their strengths to develop appropriate learning strategies.

The Disabled Students' Allowance (DSA)

In support of its commitment to encourage disabled students to enter and succeed in HE, the DfES, now DIUS established a fund which is currently administered through local authorities, the Student Loan Company (SLC) or the Open University (OU). Applications from individual students should be made to the relevant organisation (in the case of all OU students, this would be the OU, whereas other students can find out from their local authority whether to apply directly to them or to the SLC). Students on health-care courses who are in receipt of NHS bursaries should apply directly to the NHS Student Grants Unit (SGU). A copy of the Department of Health's guide 'Financial Help for Health Care Students' is available online at <http://www.nhsstudentgrants.co.uk>.

Background

The DSAs were first set up in the early 1990s, at which time there was less than £1,000 available for each disabled student, and the amount allocated to any individual was based on a needs-assessment report, generally written by a specialist dyslexia tutor or a disability officer within the student's institution. Since that time, the amount of funding has increased annually, but gaining access to the funding has often caused confusion for students as well as staff who tried to facilitate the process for students. The arrangements for awarding and distributing this funding have recently become more centralised, which should lead to a more efficient system.

Institutions are given extra government funding to help meet the needs of disabled students. The amount received varies from institution to institution, depending on the number of dyslexic students registered at the university. These figures are determined by educational reports to the Higher Education Statistics Agency (HESA) and are based on the number of students who are in receipt of DSAs. It is therefore very important for universities to have a systematic approach to eliciting and recording this information.

Accessing the DSA

In the early years of the DSA, means-testing was conducted to establish eligibility. This is no longer the case; all home students who are on recognised courses and are able to provide proof of disability are eligible for DSA awards, which are no longer means-tested. The DSA is now also available to three previously non-eligible groups: part-time students (assuming that the course on which they are enrolled is equivalent to at least 50 per cent of a full-time course); postgraduate students; and OU students. In some cases, students who received the DSA as undergraduates may reapply for further support if they enrol on a postgraduate course. This may simply consist of some funding for extra books or photocopying expenses or, in certain situations, may involve the funding of new equipment or software. Details of what is available for students who have previously received DSA support can be discussed with the needs assessor. More information about eligibility, procedures for applying and what each allowance covers can be found in the yearly publication of the DIUS, formerly the DfES, entitled *Bridging the Gap*.

Dyslexic students and those with other SpLDs must provide proof of disability, generally in the form of a diagnostic report written either by a psychologist or a specialist dyslexia teacher. The cost of this assessment is not covered by DSA funds, but institutions may use ALFs to cover all or part of the cost of the diagnostic assessment. DSA funding is available only for home students, though there is occasionally similar funding available for students from some European countries (e.g., Ireland).

Students who wish to apply for funding under the DSA must first establish their eligibility. The dyslexia coordinator or similar person at the university will usually be the first point of contact, though it is possible for a student to apply directly to the relevant local authority (or SLC or OU). In addition to the application form, the student must submit an acceptable diagnostic report conforming to the new guidance (see Chapter 2, or the DIUS, formerly the DfES, website <http://www.dfes.gov.uk/studentsupport/dsa_1.shtml>). If the report has been conducted after sixteen years of age, it should generally be acceptable, assuming that it contains the current required evidence and is not more than ten years old. If the last assessment was carried out prior to the age of sixteen, it may suffice to have an updated assessment focusing primarily on literacy attainments. The dyslexia coordinator or disability staff at the student's university should be able to advise on whether or not an existing report is acceptable.

If a student has not previously been assessed, it is necessary to have a full diagnostic report to submit with the application. The DIUS, formerly the DfES, guidance clearly states that the cost of establishing that a student has a recognised disability (in this case a SpLD) must be borne by the student. However, it may be possible for students to apply for partial or full financial assistance in meeting the costs of the diagnostic assessment (which are generally in the region of £275 to £400). Eligible students may be covered through the ALF administered through individual universities. Once again, advice should be sought from the dyslexia coordinator as to eligibility for this funding.

Once the student has an acceptable diagnostic report, this must be submitted along with the DSA application form. Assuming all information is correctly completed on the form (obtainable on the web at <http://www.direct.gov.uk/studentfinance>), the local authority (or SLC or OU) will send a letter confirming that the student can proceed to have an assessment of needs, the cost of which will be covered by the DSA. The assessment of needs is usually conducted by a trained assessor either at an independent access centre or at the university. The cost of this assessment is paid for by the DSA.

Needs assessment reports

The purpose of the needs assessment is primarily to go through the assistive technology to determine what might be relevant and helpful for a particular student as well as to explore other possible support needs.

Students often feel overwhelmed by the prospect of yet another 'assessment', and there is frequently confusion about the difference between a *diagnostic* assessment and a *needs* assessment. Whereas the former is conducted to establish that the person is, in fact, dyslexic, the latter is designed to identify and recommend appropriate support to help the student manage the effects of the dyslexia.

The needs assessment does *not* involve any testing but rather consists of a discussion with the assessor to determine what form of support will best enable the student to succeed academically. During this session, which generally lasts between an hour and a half and two hours, the student will be shown examples of the latest technology, including specialist software. After the session, the assessor will write a report containing appropriate recommendations. These recommendations generally include support in addition to specialist equipment, such as one-to-one specialist dyslexia support and possibly exam arrangement recommendations and other reasonable adjustments (for example, permission to tape lectures or the need for advanced copies of handouts).

Explanation of the allowances

The DSA is composed of three parts

1. Specialist equipment allowance. The current maximum amount for the academic year 2007–8 is £4,905 for the entire course.
2. Non-medical helper's allowance. The current maximum amount for the year 2007–8: £12,420 a year for full-time students; £9,315 a year for part-time students. This could cover the costs of a note-taker, an amanuensis (scribe) for exams or a specialist-dyslexia support tutor. (NB This does not cover subject-specific tuition.)
3. General allowance. The current maximum amount for 2007–8 is £1,640 per year for full time students and £1,230 per year for part-time students. This money could be applied to additional accessories, such as coloured paper, printer cartridges, books and photocopying.

Postgraduate students (including distance learners and relevant OU students) can apply for a single allowance to cover all costs. The current maximum amount for the year 2007–8 is £5,915.

Assistive technology

There have been many advances in technology in recent years resulting in a range of hardware and software that can prove invaluable to dyslexic people. For example, screen readers can be used to encourage improved proofreading skills. This is accomplished by enabling students to *hear* what they have written. As this is a multi-sensory strategy involving *looking* at the text while also *hearing* it read aloud, it is often easier to spot errors and to determine if the written text flows logically and states what was intended. There are many other types of software, some of which have been designed specifically for dyslexic students. (See Websites: Technology and dyslexia for a fuller description of available software.)

Developments in hardware, such as digital voice-recorders, can be extremely helpful in forging independence in the dyslexic learner. Some students feel overwhelmed by the available technology and express a kind of 'technophobia' which can affect the likelihood that recommended equipment will actually be used. It is essential that the needs assessor explores fully what the student would find helpful and also makes it clear that the DSA will cover the cost of training in using the technology, enabling students to gain confidence in the use of specialist equipment and software. Ideally, the equipment should be in place at the beginning of the course; in reality, this rarely happens, as there are several bureaucratic hoops to jump through before the recommendations are actually implemented. Unfortunately, many students feel that they don't have the time to devote to learning how to use the recommended technology, and, therefore, they may not actually take advantage of the training. It is therefore important for specialist support tutors and/or the dyslexia coordinator to encourage students to organise the recommended technology support.

Needs assessors

The expanding number of students with dyslexia and other SpLDs has resulted in large increases in the number of students applying for DSA funds. To overcome problems resulting from the lack of standardisation in needs assessment reports, the DSA Quality Assurance Group (QAG) was formed to set up a quality-assurance framework. In addition to standardising the format for reports, this group monitors the running of centres which carry out needs assessments, as well as monitoring organisations that provide equipment. (For more information about this group, see <http://www.dsa-qag.org.uk>).

A step-by-step guide to obtaining the DSA

A DSA application should be made as early as possible, preferably before the course begins, so that all support will be in place at the start of the course. The local authority (or SLC or OU) will want proof that you've been accepted on your course. If you are awarded the DSA and do not go on the course, you must return any equipment you have received to the supplier. If you do not do this, you may be liable for refunding the cost of the equipment.

1. **Obtain an acceptable (post-sixteen) diagnostic report** conforming to current standards and confirming the nature of your dyslexia.
2. **Send a photocopy of this report** along with the DSA application to the funding body (Form PN1 if you are a new student and Form PR1 if you are a continuing student). You may also apply on-line at <http://www.studentfinancedirect.co.uk>. It is best to include a copy of your full diagnostic report with your application, although it can be sent later if you apply online.
3. **Wait to receive a letter** from the relevant funding body confirming eligibility and requesting an assessment of needs.
4. **Arrange an appointment with a qualified needs assessor.** You may need to go to an assessment centre; your university might have an in-house assessment centre or an assessor might come to your university. Ask advice from your dyslexia unit.
5. Following the appointment with the needs assessor, you will generally **receive a draft copy of a report**. If you are happy with the report, the assessor will then forward it to the relevant funding body. It is then simply a question of playing the waiting game.

The speed of response from local authorities and the NHS-SGU can be extremely variable depending on the time of year, number of staff and volume of applications received. Some students must wait for a month or longer before their application is processed and an agreement for funding is received. The DSA guide *Bridging the Gap* states that 'you have a right to expect a prompt and efficient assessment of your claim' (2007: 18). It may therefore be a good idea to give a polite cough after two or three weeks, though it may sometimes take almost that amount of time to make contact with the person responsible for processing the application.

Some LAs send money directly to the individual student, while some choose to order the equipment directly from the supplier. In this case, no money is sent to you, but you must agree to third-party payments. Once the approval is given, it is usually up to you to contact the named supplier and to organise the delivery of equipment.

In some exceptional cases, you may be able to claim reimbursement for a computer already owned if you can demonstrate that it was purchased to meet your needs on a course and if you have appropriate receipts.

In some cases, you may want a higher specification machine than the one recommended in your needs assessment report or you might want an upgrade to a laptop computer if a desktop has been recommended. It may be possible to negotiate with the supplier and agree to use your own funds to pay the difference in price to get the equipment you want.

Once you have received the equipment and recommended software, it is advisable to organise assistive technology training, if this has been recommended. This may take place in your home or, in some cases, in the university, either on equipment that has the same software as you have or on your own laptop.

Other recommendations in the assessment of needs report may include one-to-one specialist learning-support sessions. These can generally be arranged through the dyslexia coordinator. Additional recommendations, including those for special examination arrangements, should also be discussed with the coordinator, who will help you implement the necessary adjustments.

Key points from Chapter 4

- Discrimination on the basis of a disability is illegal (the Disability Discrimination Act 1995 and SENDA 2001).

- HE institutions have a duty to put in place reasonable adjustments at all stages of courses, from application to completion.

- Dyslexia is classified as a disability when it affects students' ability to reach their academic potential.

- Students' need for accommodations and support varies widely, depending on the severity of their dyslexia and on their use of compensatory strategies.

- Dyslexic students may not identify with the term 'disabled', but they need to accept this nominally in order to access DSA funding.

- The DSA is not means-tested and is available to UK students, whether full- or part-time, undergraduate or postgraduate.

- The DSA funds specialist equipment, tuition and meets other costs incurred by the student as a result of dyslexia.

- A diagnostic assessment report is required as part of the DSA application process, and an assessment of need (funded through DSA) informs the provision made.

5

Dyslexia: Effects and Strategies

AUDIENCE academic staff, dyslexic students

The effects of dyslexia change over time. This is not because the condition itself has changed but because of outside influences such as educational experience and opportunities, intrinsic factors such as motivation and personality and the educational or occupational environment in which individuals are operating at any given time. However, some generalisations can be made about the sorts of tasks students with dyslexia are likely to find difficult (Snowling et al. 1997). These will be outlined in this chapter, followed by advice for both teachers and students as to how to mitigate these difficulties. The main responsibility lies with the students themselves, but some minor adjustments to teaching style and some simple accommodations on the part of teaching staff can make a very great difference.

Reading

Decoding

Skilled readers recognise words as whole units (Ehri 1995), but those who are not dyslexic are also aware, to a greater or lesser extent, of the letters that make up particular words and the order in which they appear. This enables them to notice spelling errors and to distinguish between words which look similar, for example, between 'including' and 'inducing', or 'gasp' and 'grasp'.

People who are dyslexic also recognise words as whole units; they recognise words by their overall shape, which in general works well, and many dyslexic university students have built up a very large sight vocabulary. Problems arise for them, however, when they encounter new words. Their lack of awareness of letter sequences and their difficulty converting these to sound sequences leads to a weakness in decoding unfamiliar words. In particular, they may not be able to recognise words that haven't been encountered before. What tends to happen is that students will confuse similar words such as those mentioned above or they will make an attempt at decoding and arrive at a nonsense word (for example, *egregious* becomes *egrarious*).

Dyslexic students often say that silent reading is not a problem, because the process of converting letters to sounds is bypassed. Often they will recognise the meaning of a word (or are able to make a good guess based on the context) or will know the character to whom a particular name in a novel belongs but will not be able to pronounce the word or name. Reading aloud can be very stressful because the 'bypass' is not available.

No matter how extended students' sight vocabulary may be, they constantly encounter new words during their university

> 'I used to absolutely dread reading aloud at school. When the teacher went round the class I used to spend all the time trying to work out which bit I would have to read so that I could practise it. I couldn't listen to anyone else so I ended up not knowing what was going on.'

studies. For example, the study of medicine requires students to master literally thousands of new words. This may be extremely challenging for many students, but it is especially so for dyslexic students. Most fields have specialist vocabulary which students must master, and the process of learning to recognise new words in written form so that they can be added to their sight vocabulary is particularly tricky for dyslexic students. Moreover, the intermediary stage of decoding, which comes naturally to people without dyslexia, is often almost impossible for dyslexic students.

Reading speed

Not all dyslexic students are slow readers, but the vast majority read more slowly than their peers. Whereas students who are not dyslexic may be fortunate enough to be both fast and accurate readers, for students with dyslexia there is almost always a trade-off. Those who are able to race through texts are likely to make a large number of errors and to overlook much detail; those rare dyslexic students whose oral prose reading is accurate, normally read very slowly indeed. They don't seem to be able to have it both ways.

Reading accuracy

Dyslexic people are almost always inaccurate readers. This is mainly because of their lack of awareness of detail in text, as described above. In many cases, a dyslexic student's version of a text read aloud is their own approximation, with many liberties taken with the author's script. Often this doesn't really matter, as many errors will be minor omissions of word endings or insertions of extra small function words. The meaning of the text may still be apparent so comprehension is not necessarily compromised. However, some dyslexic students make so many errors in decoding unfamiliar words and confusing similar words that they are not able fully to access the meaning of the text. In many degree courses, reading accuracy is crucial. For example, students reading law need to be aware of detail within text, as do students of pharmacology. Students of English literature also need to be aware of the actual words in texts rather than the ones they thought were written. In all subjects, the substitution or omission of a 'small' word, such as 'not', may completely alter the meaning of the text.

Absorbing information from texts

Students with dyslexia do not necessarily have comprehension difficulties. Indeed, good underlying language skills are often used to compensate for other problems in reading and writing. However, if the reading process is difficult, attention is absorbed with the reading task itself and is deflected from the processing of information, or comprehension.

Most dyslexic students say that they need to reread texts several times before they can absorb the content. They may have misread too many words fully to comprehend; they may be processing at word level rather than at sentence or text level. It may be that weakness in working memory makes it difficult to 'hold' the beginning of a paragraph, or even a sentence, resulting in the need to start again. It may even be that they are thinking about something else while reading, but this is a concentration problem which occurs as often for students who are not dyslexic as for students who are. Frequent rereading of texts is both time-consuming and frustrating and is another aspect of reading speed which needs to be recognised as a problem for dyslexic students.

Advice for teaching staff: students' reading

- **Prioritisation of reading lists**. Students may feel overwhelmed when they receive long reading lists for all their courses. Conscientious individuals may try to read every recommended text then realise that this is impossible for them. It is helpful if reading lists can be prioritised to highlight essential reading and core texts.

- In subjects involving the introduction of large numbers of unfamiliar, technical or specialist words, it is helpful if **glossaries of terms** can be provided for individual course units. Through reading the meanings of words, students are better able to distinguish between sets of words that look similar, and eventually to add them to their sight vocabulary and even to spell them.

- **Individual copies of reading materials**. Sometimes tutor groups are provided with photocopied sets of readings to share with members of the group. This can be a problem for dyslexic students, as they do not have time to complete the reading before they need to hand the photocopied set to another member of the group. Where this system operates, it is helpful if dyslexic students can be provided with their own set of readings.

- **Advice on reading strategically**. One of the problems students face with reading can be alleviated if they learn how to read selectively and with particular objectives in mind (see Tips for Students, opposite).

- **Avoid asking dyslexic students to read aloud** in class or seminars. Because their oral reading is often inaccurate, they may have experienced humiliation at school when asked to read aloud. Asking for a volunteer ensures that only those students who feel comfortable with this task will need to participate.

Tips for students: effective reading

- Decide on the objective of the reading: for example, is it for preparation for an essay, revision, preparation for tutorial, etc.?

- Think about what you already know about the subject – and about what you want to find out.

- Anticipate what might be in the text. Make a note of a few questions you think might be answered through reading the text in question.

- Survey the text: read through all the headings; read the introduction or abstract; read the first few lines of each section or paragraph; and read the conclusion.

- Remember the objectives while reading.

- Note any answers to questions posed.

- Decide whether you need to read any more – 'this may be enough'; be selective.

- If necessary, read the rest of the text in detail, highlighting key points or making notes (see note-taking advice below).

- Keep a record of all reading: full reference with a very short (50–100 words) summary of content. This will be useful for revision and for future coursework assignments.

Writing

Inaccuracy in writing

Just as one would expect students who have difficulty decoding new words to have difficulty with reflecting speech sounds in spelling, so it is to be expected that inaccurate readers will be inaccurate writers. Accuracy in writing involves spelling but also relates to punctuation, producing all the words that were intended, not repeating words and phrases and writing grammatically correct sentences. As the prose reading of dyslexic students is often an approximation of the text, so their writing is often only a version of what they intended to write. Words or whole phrases may be omitted ('when I went university'), added ('when I went to at university'); endings may be omitted ('I was think about that') or added inappropriately ('the Englished travelled'). One of the most frequently heard concerns voiced by dyslexic students is 'I know what I want to say but I can't put it down on paper'. They struggle between holding their ideas in short-term memory while trying to attend to the transcription tasks which they find so difficult (i.e. spelling, punctuation, etc.). This tension between composing and transcribing can cause considerable frustration and may result in text that fails to convey the writer's intended meaning.

Advice for teaching staff: students' writing

- **Give selective, positive feedback**. If students regularly make the same grammatical error, provide a model of the correct form of the sentence and, if possible, identify the nature of the error (e.g., no main verb, lack of agreement between subject and verb, misuse of apostrophe, etc.). It is often helpful to mark the type of error in the margin, while underlining the part of the sentence to which the notation refers. For example, rather than correct a spelling, simply write 'sp' in the margin and underline the incorrectly spelled word. This enables the student to try to identify and correct the error, which will make the correct spelling more likely to stick.

- Students should not be penalised in marking unless spelling/grammar/accuracy in English is a stated **competence standard** (see Chapter 6, Reasonable Adjustments) or if the intended meaning is not clear.

- Make sure **feedback is accessible**. Time spent in providing constructive feedback to students is wasted if the students can't decipher your comments. Ideally, feedback should be typed, particularly as dyslexic students often find it difficult to read handwritten script.

'The level of support and understanding I received from my department was very reassuring indeed. This ranged from going through my essay plans to being offered help with spelling chemical terms and expressions. As a result, the feelings of self doubt and lack of confidence were soon things of the past.'

Spelling difficulties

Whereas decoding involves converting symbols (letters) to sounds, encoding requires the conversion of sequences of sounds to letters. It is not surprising, as dyslexia involves an underlying weakness in the processing of speech sounds, that the relationship between sounds and letters is problematic in both directions.

Tips for students: Writing

- Take account of constructive feedback.

- If feedback from academic tutors indicates a problem with grammar or punctuation, this can be covered in dyslexia tuition sessions. Remember to take the piece of work to your support session.

- Plan time to leave a gap of at least a whole day between completing coursework and proofreading. Errors are more likely to be spotted with a bit of distance.

- Read work aloud when proofreading. Errors become more evident.

- Use a text reader such as 'TextHelp Read and Write' to read coursework back if reading aloud is difficult.

> 'When correcting grammatical errors or sentence structure, I have to verbalise each area to hear where I am going wrong. If the sentence still sounds wrong I search my memory for my dyslexia tutor's words explaining the errors I make. With this in mind I can more often than not put right most of the errors.'

Spelling in English is so complex that even if the skill of converting sounds to letters were to be completely mastered, not even half the battle would be won. But an ability accurately to reflect the sound structure of words in written form is a vital skill in the development of spelling knowledge. This ability is normally acquired at about six years of age and is known as the 'alphabetic principle'.

Individuals with dyslexia have difficulty acquiring this principle. From an early age, their spelling is characterised by non-phonetic spelling errors (e.g., *hlep* for *help*). Many gradually develop an ability to follow speech sounds in their writing, but then go on to have problems in applying spelling conventions and learning irregular letter patterns in English, which arguably has the most difficult written-language system. The spelling of some dyslexic students is phonetic but incorrect (for example *angsiaty* for *anxiety*), and perhaps a surprising number persist in making frequent non-phonetic errors (*enthusiasism* for *enthusiasm*, *vissitude* for *vicissitude*).

Spelling errors are often also inconsistent, with the same word spelled a number of ways in as little as one page of writing. Even word-processed work may contain errors, as homophones will not be picked up by the spell-check. Students who make non-phonetic errors often know that their attempt is wrong, but don't know how to correct it. Unfortunately, a spell-check is rarely helpful in offering suggestions for words that do not follow a reasonable phonetic approach and therefore does not help students whose spelling errors are of this nature.

Note-taking difficulties

Information processing

Taking notes in lectures is usually a relatively new skill for students coming to university and may be especially intimidating for mature students who have been away from study for a long period. The need to take notes varies from one course to another, depending on the type of handout (if any) produced. To take good notes, students must be able to listen, extract key information and write in condensed form while simultaneously listening to the lecturer. For the dyslexic student, the slow speed of language- and information-processing may make it very difficult to listen, consolidate and take down the essence of the ideas presented.

Although handwriting speed, concentration and comprehension all play a part, auditory working memory is probably the most important single factor affecting the note-taking performance of dyslexic students. This task places a heavy burden on short-term memory, as information must

---

Advice for teaching staff: students' spelling

- Marks should not be deducted for spelling errors unless it has been decided that spelling is a competence standard (see Chapter 6). This may be the case for some subjects such as English or foreign languages.

- Positive feedback. Avoid writing comments such as 'Appalling spelling!' or 'Did you check your spelling?' Most dyslexic students are very aware of their weakness in spelling and find it humiliating to receive unconstructive feedback. It is, however, helpful to identify some key words that are misspelled, to give the correct spellings and perhaps to suggest a way of remembering them. It's better to focus on a few words at a time than to cover the script with corrections.

- Suggest strategies for improving spelling, including making links between the target word and words already known; for example, start with a root word and add prefixes and suffixes, e.g., *courage, courageous, discourage, encouragement*. Other helpful strategies include using mnemonics, e.g., *diarrhoea* = '**d**ashing **i**n **a r**apid **r**ush **h**urry **o**r **e**lse **a**ccident', and identifying words within words, e.g., *piece = a piece of pie* (Jamieson and Jamieson 2003, Jamieson and Simpson 2006).

- Avoid using a red pen to make corrections. Red corrections often remind students of unhappy experiences at school when attention was focused more on errors than anything else.

'At school they used to put red pen over everything. In the end, I started writing in red, so then it didn't look so bad. Good tactic, because then my friends didn't think I was as thick as they (the teachers) were making out I was. But now I need to make sure that I never see red pens again – any other colour, but not red' *(Morgan and Klein 2000: 169).*

Tips for students: spelling

- If spelling is proving to be a particular problem, strategies for remembering keywords can be included in dyslexia tuition sessions.

- In a small notebook, compile a list of keywords and words frequently misspelled – and refer to it when writing. It is a good idea to get a small address book with alphabetised tabs. This can be used to create a personal spelling dictionary to be built up by adding words under the appropriate letters.

- Use a text reader such as 'TextHelp' to read aloud the lists of alternative words produced by the computer spell-check.

be held long enough to get it down on paper, while at the same time allowing new orally produced information to be processed. Sometimes the mere challenge of spelling a word may divert the student's attention to the extent that new information is blocked from being received. Many dyslexic students give up in despair because they find this very complex task extremely daunting.

Writing speed

Speed of writing relates to at least two different processes: first, the physical act of writing by hand and the motor skills involved; second, the process of writing combined with the process of composition. Depending on the nature of individual students' difficulties, writing speed problems may be evident in either the first or the second or both of these areas. Students who are dyspraxic (see Chapter 1) will very often have handwriting difficulties related to motor skills. Their writing is likely to be either very slow, very untidy or both, even when they do not have the additional burden of trying to plan what they want to write.

However, some dyslexic students demonstrate that they can write at a very good speed (say thirty-four words a minute) on a simple copying task but when asked to produce a piece of free writing their speed drops to about eleven words a minute. This is not a writing-speed problem *per se*; it is a result of difficulty expressing ideas in written form, and it is a very common manifestation of dyslexia in university students. Naturally, slow writing speed is a factor in note-taking, as well as in examinations. Most other required written work tends to be produced on a computer.

> 'I could probably draw or tell the information in a short format, but writing an essay takes me hours, because I find it so difficult to express myself on paper. But this hasn't spoiled my appetite to learn. I sometimes feel lost and discouraged, but I hold a picture in my mind of me in a cap and gown with my certificate in my hand.'

Advice for teaching staff: note-taking

- Provision of handouts in advance. Students with dyslexia are more likely to take effective notes and absorb the content of lectures if they have a chance to read through handouts before the lecture. They may not understand everything, but they will have a framework in mind. Ideally, at least a day in advance is helpful.

- If PowerPoint handouts are available on a departmental website, students can then annotate them during or after the lecture.

- Well-spaced handouts or handouts with three PowerPoint slides per page allow students to add to notes the lecturer has made.

- Many dyslexic students are provided with digital recorders through the DSA, primarily to serve as a back-up for note-taking in lectures. They should ask permission of the lecturer if they wish to record lectures on the understanding that recordings are solely for their personal use. The facility to listen to parts of a lecture more than once helps overcome the slow information-processing and weak auditory-memory characteristics of many dyslexic students.

- If handouts are not available in advance, it's helpful to students if a brief overview of the lecture content is given at the beginning.

'The best way I can receive information is when I listen to a tape-recorded lecture. Books and written words make my mind confused, yet when I listen to a tape I can try to envision in my own time what the lecture was about.'

Tips for students: note-taking in lectures

- Students who are receiving one-to-one teaching from a dyslexia tutor could ask for note-taking skills to be included in their teaching programme.

- Read handouts obtained in advance to provide a context for the lecture so that the content is more likely to be absorbed.

- Annotate handouts – rather than trying to write too much, add a few notes.

- Record parts of lectures. It's important, and courteous, to ask permission of tutors for the recording of lectures. When possible, record only key sections, but if the whole lecture is to be recorded, try to note the recording numbers of the sections you want to listen to again.

- Consider using a laptop for note-taking in lectures as this may save time transferring pen and paper notes later. (NB: Not all students will be funded for laptops through the DSA.)

- Write as few words as possible. Don't attempt to write full sentences as many of the words will be redundant – leave out all but the key words

- Use abbreviations (e.g., the first syllable or first few letters of words). Make sure you remember your own set of abbreviations. You might have a list of frequently used words with the abbreviations that will help you jot them down (e.g., *'bec'* for *'because'*; *'imp'* for *'important'*; *'psych'* for *'psychology'*).

- Use symbols. These can be conventional symbols such as those used in mathematics (e.g., $+$, $-$, $\times <$ etc.) or ones you have devised yourself. It is particularly useful to use abbreviated or symbolic forms for key subject words that come up time and time again – numbers can be used instead of symbols.

- Use headings or numbers when taking notes not attached to a handout. This will provide structure and make them easier to refer to later.

- Leave gaps so that if the lecturer comes back to a particular point, or if you pick up additional information when listening to the recording of a lecture, you can write your notes in the appropriate place.

- Consider mind-mapping as a note-taking technique. Multi-sensory approaches can help concentration: listening (auditory) while writing (kinaesthetic) and use of diagrams, mind-maps and colour (visual) are all valuable approaches to effective note-taking.

- Remember to sit back and listen sometimes – this may be a better way of learning.

Tips for students: taking notes from texts

- Keep the objective (revision, essay research, etc.) in mind.

- Note only relevant/key information.

- Use a system of numbering or colour coding to relate notes to objectives (e.g., essay plan).

- Make sure to take down the necessary bibliographic information, including page numbers, for any quotes you take from your reading.

- Avoid copying chunks of text in case you inadvertently plagiarise. When trying to write ideas in your own words it's better to close the book.

Number skills

Dyslexic students may have good mathematical abilities. It is important, however, to distinguish between mathematics and arithmetic computational skills, which may be an area of weakness for dyslexic people. This is related to the skills involved in computation which require accuracy, attention to detail, good sequencing and careful layout of numerical symbols on the page. Additionally, there are directional issues (understanding the meaning of computation signs such as '+' and '×' which might easily be transposed in copying). Indeed, even the language of

---

Advice for teaching staff: students' number skills

- Clarify the meanings of mathematical language.

- Give students lots of practice questions to reinforce a new concept; it may take some time and a lot of over-learning for a dyslexic student to grasp a mathematical procedure.

- Encourage students to show the working of their problems; it may then be easier to identify whether any errors are due to misconstruing the question or the concept rather than a lack of understanding of the maths.

Tips for students: number skills

- Try highlighting symbols in problems to make sure you are performing the correct operation. It is easy to get confused between an addition sign (+) and a multiplication sign (×).

- Colour code when possible (e.g., the 'x' and 'y' axes on a graph).

- Try to estimate an answer for the question so that you can determine if your final answer makes sense.

- Use mnemonics whenever possible (for example 'SOHCAHTOA' may help you to remember the angles of a triangle in trigonometry (**S**ine is the **O**pposite over the **H**ypotenuse, **C**osine is the **A**djacent over the **H**ypotenuse and **T**angent is the **O**pposite over the **A**djacent).

mathematics may be confusing to the dyslexic student. Common words take on different meanings in mathematics, which can be confusing. For example, words such as 'power', 'mean', 'proper', 'difference' and 'product' all have quite specific meanings in mathematical language. Moreover, some words combine to form a particular mathematical meaning (e.g., 'square root,' 'pie chart', 'simple interest'). A question such as 'What is the difference between 7 and 10?' may evoke a response of '3', but equally might be that one is odd and the other is even.

Oral skills

Expressive language difficulties

It is not uncommon for students with dyslexia to experience word-finding difficulties, particularly when giving presentations or in other stressful situations such as *viva voce* examinations. Again, this is linked to the phonological processing difficulty, in that words are often not very precisely stored in terms of their sound structure. They are, therefore, not reliably accessible for use in speech, which results in hesitation, perhaps the use of an alternative word or even of the wrong word. Fear that this may happen then leads to greater tension and anxiety so the problem is exacerbated. Some dyslexic students are not affected in this way at all and, indeed, much prefer to be assessed through oral rather than written communication, but it is important to identify those who have a weakness in this area so that appropriate support can be given.

> 'Being dyslexic is a fundamental part of who I am. There are many things beside reading and writing that I find difficult. I am constantly reminded of my dyslexia as I try to express myself in speech. The words I want to use vanish and I stumble, trying to find an alternative word to compensate. Often the wrong word comes out or a word that is back to front.'

Advice for teaching staff: students' oral skills

- Facilitate practice in oral presentation with peer groups.

- Allow some flexibility in regulations for note-taking during *viva voce* examinations when appropriate.

Tips for students: oral skills

- Include oral presentation skills in tuition sessions.

- Practise presenting in front of a mirror, then presenting to a friend.

- Don't use too many notes, a few bullet points in large font and key words in colour are more effective. Perhaps start off with detailed notes then gradually reduce them.

- When presenting to a group, use overhead transparencies which have the key words for the points you plan to discuss. You can then have a photocopy of the transparency on which you note the points that you wish to make to expand each of the key words.

Examinations

Dyslexic students may find examinations particularly challenging because of slow reading and writing speed, difficulty finding words and phrases to express ideas, and weakness in working memory. They are usually granted extra time in examinations and sit their exams in a separate facility with others who are having extra time. Some students are given permission to use a computer. Scripts usually have a note to advise assessors that students are dyslexic.

Advice for teaching staff: examinations

- Focus on competence standards (see Chapter 6) when marking. Students should only be penalised for weak spelling if spelling is one of the assessment criteria of the course/examination.

Tips for students: examinations

- Use most of the extra time at the beginning rather than the end to read and select questions carefully, to make notes and plan answers. If you still have time at the end of the exam, you can reread to make sure you have included all the points that you wanted. If you have omitted anything, you can include it at the end, making sure to put an asterisk at the point where it should have been.

- Remember that every word in the question is relevant.

- Plan the time carefully, according to the format of the exam. This can be done in advance. Make sure you know how long the exam is, the number of questions, whether there is more than one section, how many questions you need to answer from each section, how wide a choice there is and whether (and how) the marks are weighted.

- Monitor the time throughout the exam. Make a note of your time plan and refer back to it.

- Use the structure in the questions to structure essay answers. If possible, incorporate the question in the first sentence of your response. This will help you to focus on what is being asked.

- When planning, write down key words and any points you are afraid of forgetting. Note the main sections in order – just as bullet points.

Foreign languages

Almost all dyslexic students report having had great difficulty learning foreign languages at school, and many do not take a language at GCSE level. It makes sense that a core weakness in processing speech sounds will have an effect on learning new languages. Remembering vocabulary is a problem, especially if it is only presented orally; it is often difficult to work out where one word ends and another begins in connected speech. Oral language learning is heavily reliant on auditory working memory, which is often weak in dyslexic students. It is not surprising that dyslexic students encounter difficulty with the reading and writing modules of language courses, but it is less well understood that learning to speak and listen may also be extremely challenging.

It is unusual, though not unheard of, for dyslexic students to choose to study languages at university. Someone who has been brought up bilingually may choose to study the history or culture related to one of their spoken languages. However, fluency in spoken language skills does not preclude the fact that the student will have problems with reading and writing. Although there may be subtle differences in the effects of dyslexia on reading and writing in different languages, depending on sound–letter correspondences, the effects are still evident. In non-alphabetic languages such as Mandarin and Cantonese, the effects are likely to be less noticeable.

Many courses, such as history of art, may have compulsory language modules, so it is important for teaching staff to be aware of the problems dyslexic students may face.

Advice for teaching staff: languages

- Combine oral and written language teaching.

- To aid pronunciation, show students words written as they sound during teaching sessions.

- Make links between words that share common roots in English and the target language.

- Establish whether spelling is a competence standard and mark accordingly.

Time management

Poor time management is by no means a universal feature in dyslexia. In fact, some dyslexic students are highly organised so that their time management skills serve them extremely well as a compensatory factor. However, it is probably the case that such students are in a minority, as a very large number of students report having real difficulty estimating with any accuracy how long a given task will take. This leads to problems organising their diaries, being punctual and meeting deadlines for coursework assignments. On a different scale, poor time management can seriously affect examination performance. Students who have difficulty managing time may also have difficulty with spatial orientation and finding their way around a large campus. In general, students who experience this sort of problem may exhibit features at assessment associated with dyspraxia as well as dyslexia.

It is usually at university or college that time management becomes a major issue for the first time. At university, students are given deadlines, which they may be surprised to find are very strict. Marks will usually be lost if they miss these deadlines without prior arrangement, and extensions are not granted without good reason. On the other hand, students in higher and further education are not spoon-fed – reminders may not be given; assignments for the whole academic year, or at least for the term, may be set at once; and some projects are lengthy and cannot be completed at the last minute. Additionally, many students will be living away from home for the first time, and though they may have welcomed the thought that their parents would no longer know what they were supposed to be doing, they may have come to rely on some aspects of family support in organising their work.

Advice for teaching staff: students' time management

- Regularly remind students to read their course handbooks so that they know what lies ahead in terms of coursework deadlines.

- When possible, distribute hand-in dates evenly throughout the academic year.

Tips for students: time management

- Mark all hand-in deadlines in a diary at the beginning of the year.

- Work back from hand-in dates to plan when to start various aspects of coursework preparation and writing.

- Make a blank weekly timetable with blocks for morning, afternoon and evening for each day, including weekends. Make photocopies of it to use throughout the academic year.

- Enter taught hours and block out times for leisure/non-study. Use small Post-It notes to plan study time. If it turns out that the planned time becomes unavailable, the Post-It note can be moved to another block of free time.

- Identify study periods – but these can be swapped if necessary. Most courses assume students will spend thirty-eight to forty hours a week on their studies.

- Be realistic.

- Be flexible.

- Consider your own learning style and study in an environment that is most effective for you.

'I have to work in a room alone because I find the TV or the family talking too distracting. Also, my talking out loud so that I can hear as well as see what I'm reading distracts my family, particularly my young daughter, who thinks I'm always talking to myself.'

Key points from Chapter 5

- The effects of dyslexia may change over time, but certain patterns of difficulty are evident in dyslexic students.

- These difficulties are related, either directly or indirectly, to the core weakness underlying the individual's dyslexia, which in most cases is in the processing of speech sounds.

- Both spoken and written language may be affected.

- A major feature of the reading and writing of dyslexic students is inaccuracy.

- Speed may also be affected in either reading or writing or both, and there is often a trade-off between speed and accuracy.

- Comprehension may not be a primary problem, but reading comprehension can be adversely affected by poor reading skills, which, in turn, result in avoidance of reading.

- Organisational skills may be affected.

- Selective and constructive feedback is appreciated by students.

- Assessment of the work of dyslexic students should relate to competence standards (see Chapter 6).

- Prioritisation of reading lists is helpful.

- Any difficulties with study skills encountered by students can be addressed in their dyslexia tuition sessions.

6

Reasonable Adjustments

Background information

In 1999, the Quality Assurance Agency (QAA) produced a Code of Practice for the Assurance of Academic Quality and Standards in Higher Education, Section 3: Students with Disabilities. This document set out twenty-four precepts to which institutions in HE must adhere to ensure that students with disabilities were not disadvantaged. This Code of Practice effectively became embraced in law when Part IV of the DDA (1995) (also known as SENDA) came into effect in 2002. A subsequent amendment to SENDA which came into effect in December 2006 included new regulations in relation to public-sector agencies, including the post-sixteen education sector.

The Disability Rights Commission (DRC) has now produced a Code of Practice in relation to the 2006 DDA Amendment relating to the duties of post-sixteen education providers to prevent discrimination against existing or prospective disabled students (<http://www.drc-gb.org>).

The Code contains extensive advice which education providers must follow to ensure that they are not discriminating against disabled students. However, the status of SpLDs within the code is not absolutely clear, and students whose reports state that they are 'mildly' dyslexic may not be classified as 'disabled' if their diagnosis is deemed not to have an effect on their day-to-day lives that is 'substantial, adverse and long term'. Although the concept of 'reasonable adjustments' is fundamental to the SENDA and the 2006 Amendment, even among those dyslexic students for whom the label of 'disability' is accepted, there remains considerable confusion about what constitutes a 'reasonable' adjustment. This chapter will explore the type of reasonable adjustments which education providers in HE might be expected to provide to ensure that dyslexic students are not the victims of discrimination.

A major worry frequently voiced by academics who receive training in disability legislation is that certain adjustments might compromise 'academic standards'. In fact, SENDA specifically states that institutions are not expected to make adjustments whose effect might be the lowering of standards. The Code incorporates quite explicit information in regard to this concern.

Competence standards

'The Act defines a "competence standard" as an academic, medical or other standard applied by or on behalf of an education provider for the purpose of determining whether or not a person has a particular level of competence or ability' (Point 5.71 of the Code). Competence standards can be viewed as essential criteria which would determine admission to a particular course (e.g., playing an instrument to a certain standard to qualify for admission to a degree in music) or essential learning outcomes of a particular course of study (e.g. the ability to produce correct punctuation for a legal draft). 'A requirement that a person has a particular level of knowledge of a subject is likely to be a competence standard' (Disability Rights Commission Code of Practice, <http://drc-gb.org>).

There have been attempts to codify the action institutions must take to address situations which may disadvantage students with particular disabilities. In determining what type of adjustment might be 'reasonable' for dyslexic students, it is important to be aware that an adjustment must not, in fact, advantage dyslexic students over other, non-dyslexic, students. Therefore, it is essential to consider the underlying rationale to justify any given arrangement.

Examples of reasonable adjustments

The Code specifies the following adjustments, most of which could apply to dyslexic students in certain circumstances:

- flexible deadlines for those with variable conditions;
- support in researching booklists for those unable to 'browse' in the library;
- adjustments to assignments, such as allowing a student to submit a piece of work on video rather than in writing;
- provision of study skills support covering essay-writing or dissertation skills;
- comments on coursework in alternative formats;
- adjustments to the design or delivery of an examination;
- altering the mode of an assessment if a particular method, for example, an examination, sets up unnecessary barriers.

Alternative assessment may, in some instances, be considered as a 'reasonable adjustment' under the current legislation. The Code states that 'although an education provider has no duty to alter a competence standard, it needs to consider whether or not a reasonable adjustment could be made to some aspect of the process by which it assesses a competence standard' (Point 5.70). In some cases, there may be a justification for offering special arrangements, but it should be kept in mind that *an individual dyslexic student does not automatically qualify for an alternative assessment*. It is up to the institution, in consultation with the student and the specialist staff working with the student, to determine what, if any, changes might be appropriate. It is always the case that the adjustment must be fair both to the dyslexic student and to the non-dyslexic students on the course.

SENDA clearly states that institutions are not expected to compromise academic standards. Therefore, reasonable adjustments are intended to level the playing field but not unfairly to *advantage* any student.

Recommendations for reasonable adjustments may be suggested by both diagnostic assessors (psychologists or specialist teachers) and DSA needs assessors. However, these are only suggestions and it is normally up to dyslexia coordinators and their colleagues at individual institutions to make final decisions about adjustments, based on their knowledge of the university and individual courses.

The following list (adapted from Good Practice Guidance Notes from ADSHE and the DRC Code of Practice) provides examples of some adjustments to assessments that may be organised in particular cases. It is by no means exhaustive.

- Oral presentation of work may be allowed in the form of vivas, but both staff and students need training in the use of vivas to meet the learning outcomes of courses.
- When allowed, vivas should be recorded for external examiners.
- When recommended, students might be offered the option of presenting coursework instead of sitting examinations.
- Audio or video presentations may be allowed for students who find direct presentation difficult (e.g., due to expressive language difficulties).
- Mind-mapped presentations may be acceptable for some assessment components.
- Projects and work of a more practical kind may, in some cases, be acceptable alternatives to dissertations.
- Portfolios or presentations may be acceptable alternatives to essays.
- Short-answer responses may be an acceptable alternative to essays in some contexts.
- The use of voice-activated software in exams could be allowed for a student who relies upon and is competent in this mode of producing written work.
- The use of text-reading software should be allowed if needed.
- Exam scripts might be presented on (an agreed) coloured paper, possibly in a larger font.
- Marking of work twice for content, then for form, could be considered.
- Flexible deadlines might be agreed.
- Students who have difficulty using the library may be offered support in researching from booklists.
- Feedback on coursework might be provided in alternative formats such as on tape.

Advice for personal and academic tutors

- Make sure you know who is responsible for organising dyslexia support in your institution. Make all students aware of existing provision and encourage them to make appropriate contacts and follow existing procedures to organise special arrangements.

The nature of dyslexia is such that what is a reasonable adjustment for one person may not be appropriate for another, even if both students are on the same course. It is essential to determine what is reasonable in the context of an individual's particular difficulties, and there must be some justification for deciding on a specified adjustment. The following accommodations may constitute reasonable adjustments when an individual's cognitive profile is taken into account. The rationale for each adjustment should enable academic lecturers to think about ways in which they might adapt their courses and/or assessments to take account of the needs of dyslexic students.

Exams

Reasonable adjustment: extra time

Most UK universities have procedures for granting dyslexic students extra time on their examinations. This is commonly between ten and twenty minutes per hour, although most universities grant additional time of fifteen minutes per hour.

Rationale

One typical characteristic of dyslexia is a slow speed of processing information. This may manifest itself in slow reading, the need to spend longer processing the questions, and/or slow speed of handwriting. Many dyslexic people find it difficult to produce written work at the same speed as their non-dyslexic peers as they lack the automaticity which allows for fluent writing. The need to concentrate on the transcription aspects of writing (e.g., spelling, punctuation, handwriting, etc.) interferes with fluency of thought. It is therefore considered reasonable that extra time could compensate for these processing difficulties.

There are dyslexic students for whom extra time makes no difference; their difficulties may not be with the speed of processing but rather with inefficient working memory, which makes it very difficult for them to recall information under pressure. Usually these students will state that they don't require this accommodation. In some cases, students may require extra time for only those exams which require considerable reading and writing; exams based on numerical data may not require more time. In this event, it is the duty of the student to inform those organising exam arrangements which modules, if any, need to have the recommended extra time implemented. Some students, on the other hand, may resist special accommodations, not because they don't need them, but because they feel they will not have achieved academic success on their own merits. Discussion with dyslexia-service staff should reassure them that adjustments are made simply to take account of their dyslexia.

> 'I had a rush of pride . . . I could get by on my own merits. I did not need any help. I thought people would pity me and put all my success down to the concessions which were given to me' *(Thirty-two-year-old social-work student)*

Reasonable adjustment: separate room

Students who are granted extra time in exams should be assigned to a different room from the main cohort.

Rationale

This arrangement is intended to overcome any distractions caused by other students leaving the room earlier than the dyslexic candidate. It also minimises any embarrassment that a dyslexic student might feel when having to explain to colleagues the reason for having extra time.

Reasonable adjustment: computer

Some students with SpLDs may benefit from using a computer during exams.

Rationale

It is important to ensure that the student has a specific difficulty that results in the need to make this recommendation. Most (non-dyslexic) students for whom computers are more commonly used than pens would find it easier to produce exam scripts on a computer. However, the evidence that would justify making this recommendation for a dyslexic student is extremely slow handwriting speed and/or poor legibility of script. Students who have such problems would be disadvantaged if required to produce a handwritten document. The lack of automaticity in writing skills may mean that an individual needs to devote mental energy to thinking about how to form letters and how to ensure that the writing can be read. This will take away from the more productive activity of thinking about what to say. Freedom to use a computer overcomes the problem of the need to divert attention to the mechanical skills of writing. However, the student would need to be proficient in keyboard skills to make this a suitable recommendation.

Reasonable adjustment: software

A student who is allowed to use a computer during an exam may also be granted permission to access certain specialist software.

Rationale

If dyslexic students use software specifically intended to help them overcome their difficulties producing written work, the absence of this software may seriously disadvantage them, creating obstacles to their ability to demonstrate their knowledge in a time-constrained assessment. There are, however, important considerations to take into account before this recommendation is made. Some specialist software, such as programs designed to facilitate essay-planning, may take too much time to use in an exam situation. Even spell-checks, on which many dyslexic (and non-dyslexic) people have come to rely, take time to use. If a student is able to flag up for the marker that the script was produced by a dyslexic person, it should not be necessary to devote undue attention and time to correcting spelling. Rather, students should be given some help in learning-support sessions to develop strategies for learning to spell the more important subject-specific vocabulary that they are apt to need for their coursework and exams.

One type of software on which some dyslexic students rely is voice-recognition software, such as Dragon Dictate or Via Voice. A student who has very poor spelling and/or poor handwriting may be helped by this software which enables the user to dictate into the computer. The computer then produces a written version of what has been said, thus removing any worries about spelling and presentation. Students who have mastered this technology and rely on it to produce coursework could be disadvantaged if they are expected to generate typed or handwritten scripts. In this case, the use of voice-recognition software could be considered as a reasonable adjustment.

Reasonable adjustment: reader

Exam questions may be presented on tape, or the student can request that the invigilator reads aloud particular words or whole questions.

Rationale

Students who experience ongoing reading difficulties may be disadvantaged in exams that contain a lot of text. For example, their inaccurate reading could result in either word omissions or word additions. The omission of a 'small' word, such as 'not' could completely alter the intention of the question. Having the questions read on tape provides a multi-sensory route which should help to ensure that the intended question is understood.

Reasonable adjustment: amanuensis

Students who have significant difficulties with both reading and writing may be able to produce exam scripts with the aid of an amanuensis. The amanuensis, or scribe, literally takes the place of the student's hand – in other words, the individual acting as a scribe is not permitted to speak, other than to read back what the student has written. Additionally, the scribe could also act as a reader in cases where the student has problems with reading accuracy.

Rationale

Some dyslexic students may have severe difficulties with handwriting and/or spelling and do not have adequate keyboard skills to enable them to produce their scripts on a computer. Some students may have worked with an amanuensis when they sat GCSE or A-level exams. For those who have not had this experience, it must be kept in mind that using an amanuensis requires the mastery of additional skills, which may be difficult to acquire, particularly in a short period of time. This is not as ideal a solution as some might imagine. It requires the student to be comfortable dictating ideas aloud. The spoken sentence must conform to a style of written, rather than oral language. The natural tendency for the scribe to want to correct aspects of grammar or sentence structure must be avoided to ensure that the submitted script is written totally in the candidate's voice.

Most students who use an amanuensis for exams require practice sessions with the individual scribe so that both parties can become familiar with the style of speaking and writing. Moreover, there may be variations in what different institutions allow; for example, one university may insist that all punctuation must be dictated, while another may permit the scribe to insert the punctuation. In some cases, the student is allowed to provide a list of specialist vocabulary associated with his or her course, so the scribe does not have problems with spelling unfamiliar words. Institutions should have written guidelines on the use of an amanuensis, and both the student and the scribe should have copies of these.

Reasonable adjustment: 'flagging'

It is increasingly common for universities to have some system to flag the work of dyslexic students, particularly for examination scripts. A common system involves the use of a sticker which indicates that the student is dyslexic and may or may not request that sympathetic consideration be given to the possible effects of the dyslexia, such as weak spelling and written expression.

Rationale

In time-constrained assessments, dyslexic students do not have the same support that is available to them for coursework. For example, they will usually not have the benefit of a spell-check on the computer, nor are they likely to have the range of other technological aids on which they may have come to depend. Furthermore, they will not have the benefit of working with a support tutor to discuss ideas and arrive at a logical, sequential structure for their answer. As dyslexic symptoms are exacerbated under stress, the need to get ideas down and focus on the thinking and compositional skills can interfere with transcription skills. It is not uncommon to observe a large discrepancy between coursework results and examination results. Therefore, a sticker which states that the attached script was produced by a dyslexic student encourages markers to take into account poor spelling, handwriting and written expression when marking.

Some institutions extend the use of stickers or other flagging systems to coursework submission. However, this is a more contentious area because students who manage their time appropriately should be able to use the range of available support to ensure that their coursework is of an acceptable standard. Moreover, some students may feel that coursework submitted with a sticker requesting sympathetic marking means that they do not have to proofread or worry about spelling, punctuation, etc. This is clearly not the case, and therefore there is an expectation that, although dyslexic students may have to spend more time than their peers to produce work at the required standard, it is incumbent upon them to organise their time accordingly.

> 'The yellow stickers helped me to communicate my problem to the tutors without making a big fuss about the whole thing.'

Coursework

Reasonable adjustment: tuition

Students may receive specialist tuition to address their specific writing, spelling or reading problems.

Rationale

Learning support sessions (usually one hour per week) can be used to teach students the skills necessary to read and produce written work at an expected level for HE. Although these sessions are almost always based on actual coursework assignments, the objective of tuition sessions should be that students develop a range of skills, such as interpreting questions, planning the structure of an essay, improving grammar, sentence structure and research strategies, including understanding the conventions of academic writing, such as referencing skills. It is not the role of the dyslexia tutor to act as a proof reader, nor should tuition be subject-specific. Tutors are not expected to teach the content covered by the assignments. However, discussions and training on specialist software such as text readers can help students to identify and correct their own errors.

'The time I have with my dyslexia tutor is the most important in my week. I rarely miss a session. My tutor and I have been working on sentence structure and I am beginning to see the light at the end of the tunnel' (*Twenty-nine-year-old student teacher*)

Reasonable adjustment: extended loan time (library)

Many dyslexic students remain slow or inaccurate readers, who frequently need to reread text to extract meaning. Libraries may be able to organise extended loans, as well as special induction tours and help with understanding how to use the library, including finding information on the electronic catalogue.

Rationale

Students who are slow or inaccurate readers may find it difficult to keep abreast of the required course readings. The facility to have longer loans on borrowed books is a welcome adjustment and helps to reduce the stress created by the pressure to get through the reading within a specified time period.

Library staff can help dyslexic students maximise the benefits of using the library through separate induction tours which explain the logic of the way in which library books are catalogued and shelved. This information, which may be familiar to many students entering university, is often a sea of mystery to a student who has managed to avoid using libraries prior to university. Some universities have designated librarians who will help dyslexic students find the books or journals they need.

Reasonable adjustment: additional DSA funding

Help to access additional funding from the DSA to purchase textbooks and/or photocopy journal articles.

Rationale

Occasionally, academic lecturers may be asked to support a recommendation that eligible students be given extra funding on the DSA to cover the costs of additional books and photocopying. Although this may have been recommended in their assessment of needs, they may need to justify why they require additional books beyond those which their peers are required to purchase. Additional books might be necessary to supplement the core texts as a means of covering material in a more dyslexia-friendly way. Another reason for the need to purchase texts or to photocopy journal articles is that dyslexic students might need to highlight or annotate text to help with comprehension and retention.

Lectures

Reasonable adjustment: handouts

Provide copies of lecture notes or handouts in advance of the lecture. This enables students to familiarise themselves with the topic in advance of the lecture and should facilitate more effective note-taking.

Rationale

Note-taking in lectures is particularly difficult for many dyslexic students due to their difficulty in copying from overheads; poor short-term memory coupled with poor spelling may necessitate constantly looking at the overhead and back to the paper, and students are often unable to take down the information quickly enough. Moreover, the attention devoted to this task means they can't concentrate on the content of the lecture.

Advice for teaching staff

- Many of the adjustments that dyslexic students need can be helpful for all students. In many cases, they are simply good teaching practice and do not need to be viewed as an added burden.

Reasonable adjustment: recordings

Allow students to tape-record lectures so that they can spend more time concentrating on the talk than worrying about getting notes on paper.

Rationale

Due to the difficulties students have in taking notes, it is helpful for them to know that they can refer back to particular parts of the lecture which they have noted on their recorders. The recording is used as a back-up, but slow processing speed means that many dyslexic people need to over-learn and therefore may need to listen to something more than once.

Placements

Many degree courses include periods of time when students are engaged in work placements away from the institution. This is true for courses such as nursing, medicine, radiography and other health-care courses, as well as teaching, social work and probation. It also covers many courses in business, in which students may elect to spend a 'sandwich year' in which they gain valuable work experience prior to completing their final degree year. Many other courses also have some period when students are engaged in more practical activities outside of the university, such as field trips.

Disclosure and confidentiality

The DDA applies to work environments as well as education, but many dyslexic students are concerned that disclosing their 'disability' to prospective employers or placement supervisors may jeopardise their chances either of getting the placement or of success. The university has a responsibility to maintain confidentiality unless the student has agreed to disclosure. In some cases, the practical aspects of a placement do not present any difficulties to the dyslexic learner, and therefore there is no need to inform the practice supervisor that the student is dyslexic. However, many placements require students to perform a variety of tasks such as writing reports, maintaining records, taking minutes at meetings or drafting letters. Such tasks may tap into the student's weaknesses and potentially create a problem unless the supervisor or mentor is aware of the student's specific learning difficulty. It is therefore a good idea for students to discuss disclosure with their personal or academic tutors to arrive at a decision as to whether it would be appropriate to inform their placement supervisor of their dyslexia.

> 'Some students might not disclose their disability because they fear discrimination. It is important to reassure them that this is not the case and briefly explain the benefits to the student of disclosing their disability.'

Students must remember that, in the event they decide *not* to disclose, placement staff may not be in a position to put in place reasonable adjustments. Therefore, in cases where a student feels it is necessary to have adjustments to ensure best performance on the placement, it would be wise to encourage disclosure. One reasonable adjustment that could be arranged for students on placement is that they are granted time off to attend dyslexia-support sessions. This could be beneficial, particularly in terms of developing coping strategies to meet the demands of the placement.

The disclosure of dyslexia by a student is entirely a personal decision. However, the institution has to give the student opportunities to disclose in a range of contexts. Often the likelihood of a student disclosing will depend on the institutional ethos. Therefore, dyslexia-support staff should assure students that confidentiality will be maintained, and it is the student's choice as to whether or not to inform lecturers or anyone else that they are dyslexic. Moreover, as it would be a breach of confidence for the dyslexia coordinator or any other member of dyslexia/disability services to communicate information about a particular student without consent, it is advisable to have students sign a form to grant permission for any communication from the dyslexia unit which the student requests. For example, if students want to have special examination arrangements put in place, it may be necessary to involve examination officers, the Registry, the academic department and possibly others. (Sample confidentiality and disclosure forms are available in the resources section and on the CD.)

Once a student agrees to disclose a disability, the institution is deemed responsible for putting in place reasonable adjustments. The Code states that institutions should have a 'confidentiality policy which ensures the information will not be misused and gives applicants confidence in the system' (DRC Code, Point 8.38). There should also be procedures to ensure that when a student decides to disclose to non-specialist disability staff (such as personal tutors, librarians and exams officers), information is given to the student about referral processes and details should be passed on as appropriate with the student's permission.

> 'I think being more aware of what counted as a disability would encourage other students to come forward, as after disclosing help can be put in place straight away' (*Nineteen-year-old geography student*)

Students not in receipt of DSA funding

The Code makes it clear that the duty of HE institutions to provide a system of reasonable adjustments applies equally to all students with disabilities. Moreover, it covers students from the time of applying for a course to after they complete the course. Furthermore, institutions have an anticipatory duty to put systems in place to cover the eventuality of a student with a particular disability attending the university, even though there might not be any students with that disability currently in attendance. For example, institutions should consider alternative procedures for programmes which include an admissions interview, in cases where a speech difficulty, such as a severe stammer, might disadvantage a student.

Although DSA funding can help individual students who have an acceptable diagnostic report confirming the nature of their dyslexia, this funding is available only to home students who are enrolled on approved courses. If may not, for example, apply to a student on a short course. However, the Code states that European and international students have the same rights as home students. Therefore, it is incumbent upon institutions to consider how to implement reasonable adjustments in the case of students who are not DSA-funded.

Key points from Chapter 6

- The concept of 'reasonable adjustments' remains subject to interpretation.

- The objective of putting adjustments in place is that students should reach their academic potential.

- Reasonable adjustments should not compromise academic standards.

- Adjustments will vary according to the effects of dyslexia on individual students.

- Adjustments may relate to examination arrangements, coursework, library regulations, teaching, placements and field trips.

- Students need to disclose their dyslexia if the appropriate range of reasonable adjustments is to be put in place.

7

Roles and Responsibilities

AUDIENCE dyslexic students, academic staff, dyslexia tutors

Models of dyslexia and disability services

Dyslexia services within disability services

The way in which dyslexia support is incorporated into the overall structure of a university varies according to the institution. For example, some universities offer dyslexia support as part of a wider student-services provision. There may be a separate unit within student services with a designated responsibility to provide support for dyslexic students and, perhaps, those with other SpLDs such as dyspraxia, dyscalculia and ADD/ADHD and Asperger Syndrome. There is often a close affiliation between the general disability support service and the dyslexia support service; indeed, in some institutions, dyslexia support is situated within the wider disability remit. However, in recognition of the fact that many dyslexic students do not consider themselves to have a 'disability' and may, therefore, be reluctant to approach disability services for help, the dyslexia support unit is often a separate entity.

Dyslexia services within learning/language support

Another common model is that which views support for dyslexic students as one aspect of the general academic support provision open to all students. This model tends to link dyslexia support with general language or learning support, including study skills and possibly language support for non-native speakers. The overarching department in this case may be an educational development unit or simply a language support unit.

Dyslexia services within the academic framework

A third model which is less common than the others involves having a named person within a faculty or department who assumes responsibility for disabled students. Usually, this person becomes a link between the student and the academic tutors within the department. This model may be less efficient than the other two, particularly when students take modules across different faculties.

Accessing support

Although the structure of dyslexia support may vary across institutions, the nature of the specific support provided to dyslexic students will generally be similar. It is important that students find out what support is available and how it is organised within their institution and what arrangements they must make to ensure that their needs are identified and addressed. Unfortunately, the initial barrage of information to which new students are subjected is often so overwhelming that they forget to register early in the term. It is not uncommon for students who have had extra time at GCSE and/or A-levels to expect that the same arrangements will automatically be put in place for them at university as long as they have ticked the appropriate box on their enrolment form. In fact, this is not the case; rather, it is up to individual students to find out not only what procedures they must follow to organise special arrangements but also to be aware that there are usually deadlines for making these arrangements. It is not unusual for dyslexia coordinators to receive frantic last-minute pleas for extra time in exams from students who have not considered that there are procedures, including deadlines, set up to organise these arrangements, and they simply can't be put in place at the last minute. A registration/disclosure form which can be customised for individual institutions is included in the resources section and on the CD. There are also forms for notifying academic and other relevant staff that individual students are dyslexic.

> **Student tip:** *Find out how to register with the dyslexia support service as early in your first term as possible – you can find information about the support service by looking at the university website. Also make sure you know about any deadlines for organising special examination arrangements.*

Obligations of the university

SENDA makes it incumbent upon institutions to provide support to those students who have declared a disability, including a SpLD (see Chapter 4 for a fuller explanation of the legislation). In practical terms, any student who has ticked the box for disability either on a Universities and Colleges Admissions Service (UCAS) form or an enrolment form is deemed to have informed the university of the existence of a disability. The onus is therefore on the university to make contact and to encourage the student to register with the appropriate unit so that the process of organising support can begin.

Students new to HE are often overwhelmed by trying to navigate the complex bureaucratic structures which characterise most large organisations. This may be particularly true for mature students who have returned to education after a long gap and who may find the whole process quite daunting. Equally, 'traditional' students who enter university following their A-levels may be disappointed in the lack of personal attention to which they were accustomed at school and/or college.

It is particularly important for dyslexic students to organise their support as soon as possible after they begin their courses, as they might easily fall behind, and, if they don't receive the support they need, they might struggle to succeed in their first year. Therefore, specialist dyslexia tutors as well as academic tutors and exams officers must liaise to inform students what procedures they must follow. Staff should appreciate that the nature of dyslexic difficulties often includes poor organisational skills, resulting in students not always following procedures which have been set up. This is not intentional neglect; rather, it is more likely a response to information overload. It is therefore crucial that relevant departments within the university establish communication channels to ensure that information about student needs is shared and appropriate action is taken. This might entail the registry sending information to the dyslexia-support service regarding the names of newly enrolled students who have indicated that they have a SpLD. This enables the dyslexia-support service to contact the student and set necessary steps in motion.

> *Advice to Staff: Make sure that systems are in place to ensure that there is clear communication between the dyslexia-support service and named people in relevant departments, such as the registry, the exams office and academic departments. Remember that it is up to the university to notify students with SpLDs about procedures for putting necessary support in place. This includes having information easily available to students on the university website, student handbooks and the university prospectus. It is also advisable to make personal contact with every student who has self-identified at enrolment.*

Who is likely to provide what help?

Part of the confusion faced by students new to university is caused by not knowing whom they can approach for help. Many people in different roles assume responsibilities designed to make the transition to degree-level study easier. However, the very fact that sources of important information or help are fragmented in terms of their physical location and between academic and non-academic departments can create inertia in the student as a result of not knowing where to begin. People occupying the following roles are usually important sources of information/

The dyslexia coordinator

The person in charge of organising provision for dyslexia support is usually a good initial contact. This is particularly relevant for students who arrive at university with an existing diagnostic assessment. Usually, the dyslexia coordinator will have contacted students who have identified themselves as dyslexic on either UCAS or enrolment forms. An initial meeting with this person will clarify procedures which must be followed to organise:

- special examination arrangements;
- application for DSA;
- specialist dyslexia support;
- communication, when appropriate, with academic tutors;
- implementation of any other reasonable adjustments related to the specific nature of an individual's problems;
- other existing provision within the institution (e.g., library accommodations, special computer facilities).

Students who are concerned about the difficulties they encounter with learning but who have not previously been diagnosed as dyslexic may also approach the dyslexia coordinator who may be able to organise an initial screening.

> *Student Tip: Make sure to arrange an appointment with the dyslexia coordinator as soon as possible. Remember to take a photocopy of your most recent diagnostic assessment – to be acceptable for purposes of DSA, it must have taken place after you were sixteen. If you have never been assessed, but would like more information, then the dyslexia coordinator may be able to arrange a screening to determine if a full assessment is appropriate.*

The dyslexia coordinator may also have a staff-development brief. This includes ensuring that there is awareness about SpLDs among staff as well as advising the institution about compliance with current disability legislation.

The diagnostic assessor

Increased awareness about dyslexia has resulted in a growing number of students who are concerned about the difficulties they face with academic study. As it would not be possible to conduct full diagnostic assessments for every student who voiced some concern about learning, most institutions have a system for an initial screening to determine whether a full diagnostic assessment is indicated. If the student has a positive screening, it is likely that a referral will then be made to a qualified assessor (see Chapter 2 for more details of what is involved in the screening and diagnosis of dyslexia).

Some universities may employ staff who are qualified to diagnose dyslexia or may be able to refer students to a suitable assessor. The assessor will be either a chartered psychologist or a specialist dyslexia tutor with a practising certificate in assessment. Although the certificate does not specify an age range, it is expected that professionals who assess university students have training and experience in this field. The assessor will usually conduct a full diagnostic assessment (see Chapter 2 for details), write a comprehensive report and make general recommendations for the type of support the student needs.

The cost of diagnosis is not the responsibility of the institution; if a student wants a full assessment, the cost could vary from approximately £275 to £400. However, some universities may point the student in the direction of funding which might cover all or part of these costs. In particular, many universities are able to fund assessments for home students through the ALF.

> **Student Tip:** If you are concerned about the difficulties you experience with academic work, contact the dyslexia coordinator at your university to request a screening for dyslexia.

The disability coordinator

The role of the disability coordinator varies according to the structure of the institution. In some universities, the person in this role has overall responsibility for all disabilities, including SpLDs, so in some cases, there is only one person acting as disability/dyslexia coordinator. There may be a team of people who are managed by this coordinator who will delegate responsibility to the relevant person/s depending on the needs of an individual student.

In addition to overseeing the running of the disability service, the disability coordinator may also have responsibility for ensuring that university disability policies are in line with current legislation. Another part of this role may be a staff development brief to keep academic and other university staff (e.g., the examinations office, library and computing services, careers service) abreast of their legal responsibilities in relation to providing for the needs of disabled students.

Regardless of the precise breakdown of responsibilities between the dyslexia and disability coordinators, it is generally the case that the people occupying these two roles work closely together to ensure that student needs are met. Furthermore, an individual dyslexic student may have other disabilities, and, although willing to have his or her dyslexia noted, may prefer to have another disability remain confidential. The pros and cons of this decision can be discussed in confidence with the disability coordinator to arrive at a satisfactory solution.

> **Student Tip:** *If you have a disability in addition to being dyslexic, you may want to make an appointment with the disability coordinator to discuss this. You have the right to ask for the information you provide on any disability to remain confidential.*

The dyslexia tutor

Once a student has been diagnosed as dyslexic, it is usually possible to arrange one-to-one or small group tuition to address strategies that might be helpful for improving academic work. Although universities are not required to provide specialist dyslexia tutors to support individual students, it is increasingly common for dyslexia support services either to have existing specialist tutors who work as part of the support team or to be able to put students in touch with a qualified tutor who can provide support on a private basis.

The non-medical helper's allowance of the DSA can fund the costs of specialist dyslexia tutors. In some instances, it may be necessary for the student to have received approval of DSA funding prior to the university making these arrangements. If specialist tutors are not engaged directly by the university, the student might need to find a tutor who is willing to invoice the local authority directly to cover the cost of teaching. Fees range from about £35 to £60 per hour, but the expected figure is usually specified in the student's needs assessment report. (More information about this can be found under the discussion of the DSA in Chapter 3.) A tuition record form and a tuition session evaluation form are included in the resource section and on the CD.

Learning support

In general, the dyslexia tutor provides learning support tailored to the needs of individual students. For example, if a student is having difficulty with reading, reading strategies will be explored using the course materials as a basis for discussion. Likewise, essay-writing skills may be taught in relation to a particular coursework assignment, such as an essay. The tutor will explore with the student the existing strategies being used and suggest others which might be more appropriate to the student's learning style. Learning support sessions might also focus on understanding the individual's learning style or on enabling students to gain a better insight into the effects of dyslexia on their individual learning, literacy and study skills.

In addition to addressing difficulties with reading, writing, spelling, note-taking and exam revision, learning-support sessions might also focus on time management and organisational skills. Some students need more regular sessions than others, and, indeed, many decide that they can manage without tuition. Sometimes the needs assessment indicates the

> 'Support sessions are invaluable to dyslexics; without them you remain alone and lost in the incomprehensible jungle of written communication – without map, compass or direction. I know – I was lost. How do sessions help? First, they help identify the problems you have – the map. Second, they arrange work patterns to help you counteract the effects of the disability – the compass. Third, by constant encouragement, understanding and advice, they help you find a way out of your difficulties – the direction' (*KM, first-year LLB student, age thirty*)

number of hours that will be funded, but applications for further funding can be made if the tutor and student agree that this is necessary.

> **Student Tip:** *Try to arrange learning support sessions early in your course. Do not make the mistake of thinking that you don't have time to attend support sessions – the strategies you learn may save you time in the long term.*

The personal tutor

Most courses assign students to a personal tutor within their academic department. The main role of a personal tutor is to provide students with the support they need to achieve their academic goals. This may entail help with any problem that impinges on the student's learning. In addition to academic difficulties, the personal tutor might also refer students for help with personal/emotional or financial difficulties.

However, as the number of students in HE continues to grow, it is becoming increasingly common for students to be assigned to a group who meet the personal tutor together. This may make it difficult for dyslexic students who might require more time to process information. If this is the case, it is important for personal tutors to be made aware of the needs of individual students. This can be accomplished either by the student making an individual appointment to discuss his or her needs as well as to explain the effects dyslexia may have on his or her academic work. If a student feels uncomfortable with such a direct approach, it might also be possible, with the student's permission, for the dyslexia coordinator or the student's dyslexia-support tutor to liaise with the personal tutor. This contact could clarify the needs of a particular student, as well as acquainting the personal tutor with the issues faced by dyslexic students and reinforcing the importance of appropriate teaching strategies and accommodations. Because of the confidential nature of information held by the dyslexia-support services, any communication between them and other branches within or outside the institution will take place only with the student's knowledge and consent.

The academic tutor

Often students find it difficult to identify exactly where their problems lie. They may approach a learning-support session saying that they need help in structuring an essay, but, in reality, the problem is more about their lack of subject understanding. As it is not the role of dyslexia-support tutors to provide subject-specific tuition, they will often refer students back to the academic tutor for help with understanding subject content. Indeed, it is often the case that dyslexic students feel embarrassed about their difficulties but may discover that many of their peers are equally confused about a particular topic or assignment. The problem may lie in the presentation of the topic or in a lack of clarity in the assignment brief. In this case, the appropriate course of action is to approach the academic tutor for clarification. If the tutor is aware that a particular student is having difficulty with course content, it may be possible to recommend a postgraduate student who could provide some additional tuition. However, this is completely separate from the nature of dyslexia support, and any costs incurred would have to be borne by the student.

If an academic tutor is aware that a student is dyslexic, it is reasonable for the student to expect that certain reasonable and recommended adjustments are put in place. These might include allowing the student to record lectures and/or seminars, providing advance copies of lecture notes and/or handouts or setting aside some time to look over the first draft of a student's essay.

Student Tip: *Make sure you understand the different roles assumed by different people. Take advantage of the support available, but remember that it is up to you to seek advice and help. Do not leave it to the last minute, because then it may be too late.*

Responsibilities of the student

Although universities must offer reasonable adjustments to disabled and dyslexic students to enable them to demonstrate their full potential, this does *not* mean that you can sit back and expect all arrangements to be put in place automatically. On the contrary, you must act to ensure that appropriate arrangements have been implemented. In particular, there is usually a deadline for putting examination arrangements in place, and this is likely to be several weeks before the beginning of the examination period. It is therefore essential that you take the following actions:

Establish contact

Find out who is responsible for organising dyslexia support. This information may be available in the university prospectus, in the course handbook and/or on the university website. Arrange an appointment to meet the relevant person to organise your support needs. You should take with you a photocopy of your most recent diagnostic report, which will be kept with your records in the dyslexia support service. The dyslexia-coordinator will advise you whether this report is acceptable or whether you will need to have a more recent assessment.

Find out about the Disabled Students' Allowances (DSA)

See Chapter 4, pp. 27–32.

Examination Arrangements

Make sure you know what you must do to implement any special examination arrangements which have been recommended for you. These *will not* automatically be in place unless you have informed the relevant department (usually the exams office) which exams you will be taking. Since this information changes for each examination period, you may be responsible for communicating your needs *each time*. For example, there may be occasions when you feel you do not need extra time (possibly for a maths assessment which has little or no writing requirement), and you can then sit the exam with the rest of your cohort.

'The disability department was enormously helpful and encouraging to me in making my application to my local authority for an assessment of my needs. As a consequence I have an excellent laptop and other items of equipment which are proving a real asset.' (*FJ, business studies student*)

Form-filling

Familiarise yourself with any forms you must complete and seek help from the dyslexia unit if you are unsure about what is expected of you.

Diary

Make a note in your diary for any important information, such as the deadline for submitting examination forms or dates for learning support.

Follow-up

If you are having difficulty with your DSA application, make sure you seek advice. This may be from the dyslexia unit, or possibly from a student welfare adviser, who might be able to contact the local authority on your behalf. Do *not* sit back and wait: sometimes applications get lost, so it is important to chase up a DSA application if you have not had any response after a period of, say, one month.

International students

Whereas much of the above information is relevant to home students, overseas dyslexic students who are not eligible for DSA may still expect support from their universities. This support will generally entail examination arrangements, but there may also be some provision through the general language-support department for help with study strategies. Some institutions have a specialist dyslexia tutor who works in the language-support department and is available for general study skills for all students, but who can also provide some specialist help to dyslexic students. Some provide funding whereby specialist technology can be made available as a loan for the duration of the course.

> **Student Tip:** *Be proactive. Make sure that you have contacted the relevant people within the university and that you follow up to make sure that recommended adjustments have been put in place for you.*

Key points from Chapter 7

- The administration of dyslexia services varies from one university to another, but in most cases there is a strong link between dyslexia and disability services.

- Most institutions have a disability coordinator and a dyslexia coordinator, but in some cases these roles are combined. Other relevant staff include diagnostic assessors, dyslexia tutors, personal and academic tutors.

- Although universities have a duty to make contact with students registered as having a disability, students should be proactive in making themselves known to the dyslexia-service staff.

- It is important for students to make contact with the disability/dyslexia service staff at an early stage to ensure that appropriate support and accommodations are put in place.

CD and photocopiable resources

This section of the book contains a number of resources that have been developed to be used by dyslexia/disability services staff. These resources can be photocopied directly from the book or can be downloaded onto a computer from the CD. The templates can be personalised for use in different institutions. These are:

1. Student registration document (dyslexia/disability services)

This document is for use in dyslexia/disability centres and includes a disclosure/confidentiality statement.

2. Permission to disclose personal information

This is a separate disclosure form which may be suitable for some administrative systems.

3. Notification of student's registration as dyslexic

This is a simple form for students who have a previous diagnosis of dyslexia but who have not been assessed by the university dyslexia staff. Its purpose is to notify teaching and library staff of a student's dyslexia at the beginning of their course, and basic recommendations for support are made. Copies of this form can be attached to the student's coursework assignments.

4. Confidential information for academic/library staff

This sheet can be used as a template and personalised for individual students. It is divided into two parts: the effects of dyslexia on literacy and study skills (which needs to be personalised for the individual) and recommended support from the academic department. Any factors that do not apply to a specific student can be deleted. Copies of these sheets can be attached to a student's coursework assignments.

5. Application for support from the HE Access to Learning Fund (ALF)

The standard application form for ALF is unnecessarily detailed, complex and lengthy for the purpose of requesting funding for diagnostic assessments for dyslexia. For example, it is not necessary for students to provide information about their financial status. This is an adapted form, which the DfES, now DIUS has deemed acceptable for the purpose.

6. ALF application (alternative form) 2

7. Student questionnaire (screening/background to assessment)

This questionnaire elicits useful background information about students for assessors or staff administering screening tests. It covers developmental, educational and assessment history, and students' current concerns about their literacy and study difficulties

8. Dyslexia tuition record form

Local authorities generally require written records of tuition sessions received by students, signed by the student and the tutor before payment to the tutor or institution can be made. This form can be submitted at the end of each term or after a certain number of tuition sessions as appropriate.

9. Dyslexia tuition evaluation form

This form is for the use of tutors and their students. It can be completed in a few minutes at the end of each session to focus attention on learning outcomes and future needs.

Student Registration Document

Name:	ID number:
Course:	Department:
Start Date:	Postgraduate/Undergraduate:
	Full/Part-time:
End Date:	Home/EU/Overseas:
Home Address:	Term-time Address:
Home Tel:	Term-time Tel:
University E-mail:	Disability:
Personal E-mail:	

The Dyslexia/Disability Centre has written evidence of my disability ☐

© Claire Jamieson and Ellen Morgan (2008) *Managing Dyslexia at University*, Oxon: Routledge

Disclosure and Confidentiality

All information passed to the Disability Centre about individual students is kept confidential. This information is confidential personal information and covered by the Data Protection Act. In order to make the adjustments that you might need and to put support in place it may be necessary to pass information to other parts of NAME OF UNIVERSITY (for example your academic department, the Examinations Section, the library). This will be done only with your express permission.

I agree that information about my disability may be passed to others at NAME OF UNIVERSITY **on a need to know basis.**	**YES / NO***

*If you do not want any information to be passed on this may affect what adjustments can be made and what support can be put in place. If you would like information about your disability to be passed on to your department the DYSLEXIA/DISABILITY CENTRE will do this by way of completing an individual support summary with you. An appointment will be made for you with a member of the DYSLEXIA/DISABILITY staff to discuss your support. At the end of your appointment you will be given a copy of the support summary which you can then pass on to your personal tutor and other members of staff in your department for whom it is relevant.

Please tick the box if you would like to arrange an appointment: ☐

Office Use

Date of Appointment:

Summary Form on File: ☐

Please indicate which of the following you think you may need or would like to find out more about:

Dyslexia Diagnostic Assessment		Screening/Up-date
Dyslexia Tuition		
Help with Proofreading		
IT Training		
Note-taking Support		
Extended Library Loan		Date of request to library:
Insert more rows as required		
Other (please state):		

© Claire Jamieson and Ellen Morgan (2008) *Managing Dyslexia at University*, Oxon: Routledge

Disabled Students' Allowances (UK Home students only):

Some of the support services mentioned above may be dependent on your receiving Disabled Students' Allowances (DSA). It would be helpful for us to know whether you are applying for DSA and if so, what stage your application is at. Please tick as appropriate:

		Notes:
I have not applied for DSA but would like to find out more		
I have applied to my LEA/funding council		
I have been for an Assessment of Needs		
My application was turned down		
I do not intend to apply for DSA at this stage		
Name of LEA/Funding Council:		

Special Exam Arrangements

Do you intend to apply for special exam arrangements?   ☐ Yes   ☐ No   ☐ Not sure

Institution-specific information

Sign:	Date:
Notes:	

© Claire Jamieson and Ellen Morgan (2008) *Managing Dyslexia at University*, Oxon: Routledge

UNIVERSITY LOGO/
LETTERHEAD

DYSLEXIA/DISABILITY SERVICES

Permission to Disclose Personal Information

Name: _____

ID Number: _____

E-mail:_____

Course: _____

Start Date: _____ Finish Date:_____

I understand that all information held about me by the DYSLEXIA CENTRE/UNIT is confidential and will only be disclosed to relevant parties at my request and/or with my knowledge.

I consent to information being disclosed to the following, as appropriate:

☐ ALL   ☐ Examinations Office

☐ Academic Department   ☐ Library Information Service

☐ Access Centre   ☐ Student Union Advice Centre

☐ Local Authority   ☐ NHS Funding Council

☐ Accommodation and Welfare Service   ☐ Other_____

Signature:_____

Date:_____

© Claire Jamieson and Ellen Morgan (2008) *Managing Dyslexia at University*, Oxon: Routledge

UNIVERSITY LOGO/
LETTERHEAD

DYSLEXIA/DISABILITY SERVICES

Notification of Student's Registration as Dyslexic

A copy of this page can be attached by the student to written assignments

Student's Name

ID Number

Degree Programme

Year

The above student is registered as dyslexic with DISABILITY CENTRE and has provided a copy of his/her diagnostic assessment report.

Support/accommodations, which can be put in place immediately, include:

- extended borrowing time from libraries;

- provision of handouts before lectures;

- permission to record lectures/key parts of lectures;

- adherence to NAME OF UNIVERSITY guidance on assessing the work of dyslexic students (WEBSITE REFERENCE).

Signature of dyslexia coordinator

Signature of student

Date:

© Claire Jamieson and Ellen Morgan (2008) *Managing Dyslexia at University*, Oxon: Routledge

Confidential Information for Academic Library Staff

Student's Name:

Department:

Degree Course:

Year:

NAME has been diagnosed/confirmed as dyslexic following an assessment on DATE

_____'s dyslexia has the following effects on his/her literacy/study skills:

- ☐ slow reading speed
- ☐ inaccurate reading
- ☐ slow handwriting speed
- ☐ difficulty proof-reading
- ☐ difficulty absorbing information from texts

- ☐ spelling/punctuation difficulties
- ☐ difficulty expressing ideas in writing
- ☐ difficulty expressing ideas orally
- ☐ difficulty with grammar

Recommended support

- ☐ provision of handouts in advance of lectures when possible
- ☐ permission to record key parts of lectures
- ☐ extended borrowing time from college libraries
- ☐ individual induction session for library
- ☐ help with proofreading
- ☐ A recommendation for extra time in examinations (minutes an hour)

Teaching staff should refer to the NAME OF UNIVERSITY guidance

for assessing the work of dyslexic students (WEBSITE)

Student's signature: _____

Dyslexia coordinator: _____

© Claire Jamieson and Ellen Morgan (2008) *Managing Dyslexia at University*, Oxon: Routledge

UNIVERSITY LOGO/
LETTERHEAD

DYSLEXIA/DISABILITY SERVICES

Academic Year 200—/200—   **Date of Receipt**

Application for support from the
HE Access to Learning Fund (ALF)
for Dyslexia Diagnostic Assessment ONLY

Important

If you wish to apply to the fund for assistance with anything other than a dyslexia diagnostic assessment you will need to complete a full application form.

Part 1 Your Personal Details

1.	Student Number						
2.	Title (tick one box only)	Mr		Mrs		Miss	
		Ms		Other			
3.	First Names (in full)						
4.	Surname (in full)						
5.	Gender	Male		Female			
6.	Date of Birth (DD/MM/YYYY)						
7.	Age						
8.	Your Full Correspondence Address	Term-time		Home			
		Postcode		Postcode			
9.	Telephone Number						
10.	E-mail Address						

© Claire Jamieson and Ellen Morgan (2008) *Managing Dyslexia at University*, Oxon: Routledge

Part 2 Academic Details

11.	Programme Title						
12.	Department						
13.	Level of Study			Undergraduate		Postgraduate	
14.	Are you studying	Full-time		Part-time		Distance Learning	
15.	Year of Study	1		2		3	4	Other (please state)	
16.	Is this your final year?			Yes		No	
17.	Is this a repeat year of study?			Yes		No	
18.	If part-time, please state the number of course units/modules/credits being taken						

Part 3 Disability/Special Medical Needs

20.	Do you have a disability or chronic medical condition?	Yes		No	
21.	Have you applied for a disabled students' allowance (DSA)?	Yes		No	
22.	Do you wish to apply for financial assistance towards any special equipment/material not covered by a DSA or for assistance towards the cost of a diagnostic test (for a specific learning difficulty, e.g., dyslexia)?	Yes		No	

© Claire Jamieson and Ellen Morgan (2008) *Managing Dyslexia at University*, Oxon: Routledge

Confidentiality

> Applications are seen only by .... It may be necessary for additional supporting information to be sought from other university staff in order for the Committee to reach a decision.

Data Protection Act 1998

> NAME OF UNIVERSITY is a data controller in terms of the 1998 legislation. Student Financial Support follows NAME OF UNIVERSITY policy in matters of data protection. The data requested in this form is covered by the notification provided by NAME OF UNIVERSITY under the Data Protection Act. Personal data will be used to administer your award as appropriate, and for statistical purposes and electronic record keeping.
>
> The data will not be passed to any other third party without your consent, except when NAME OF UNIVERSITY is required to do so by law. Any formal enquiries concerning the use of data noted here should be addressed to the NAME OF UNIVERSITY Data Protection Officer.

Part 10 Declarations

Please read the following declarations and sign and date.	
I declare that the information that I have given on this form is correct and complete to the best of my knowledge. I understand that giving false information will automatically disqualify my application and may also lead to disciplinary procedures resulting in possible expulsion from NAME OF UNIVERSITY. I further undertake to repay any funding obtained by me as a result. I also confirm that I have read the guidance notes.	
Signature	
Date	

For Office Use Only

Initial Decision	
(sign)	
Date	
Checked (initials)	
Date	
Category of Award	
Application Number	

© Claire Jamieson and Ellen Morgan (2008) *Managing Dyslexia at University*, Oxon: Routledge

ACCESS TO LEARNING FUND (INSERT YEAR)

General Information to be completed by student:	OFFICE USE ONLY
Name: _____	
Course and Year: _____	Date Received:
Age and Date of Birth: _____	
Address: _____	
_____	HESA No:
_____	
_____	
	_____
Contact Tel No: _____	Approved by Dyslexia Co-ordinator:

Completed forms should be returned to DEPARTMENT with a photocopy of the invoice for the dyslexia diagnostic test.

Have you previously applied to the Access to Learning Fund in this academic year?   YES / NO

Date:

Information about assessment appointment and any financial implications of failure to attend

_____

Date of Test:

Charge:

To be eligible for the Access to Learning Fund to pay the assessment cost you must meet residency and other conditions. Overseas students and non-UK EU students (including those who are eligible for tuition fee support) cannot apply to the Access to Learning fund. As well as meeting residency conditions you must be a full or part time student (studying at least 50 per cent of a full time course) on a course of Higher Education.

It is not possible to list here all the criteria. If we do not think you meet all of the requirements for funding we will contact you as soon as possible for more information.

© Claire Jamieson and Ellen Morgan (2008) *Managing Dyslexia at University*, Oxon: Routledge

YOU MUST SIGN THE DECLARATION BELOW

- I declare that the information that I have given on this form is correct and complete to the best of my knowledge.
- I understand that giving false information will automatically disqualify my application and may also lead to disciplinary procedures resulting in possible expulsion from the University. I further undertake to repay any financial awards obtained by me as a result.

Your Name (CAPITALS): _____

Your Signature: _____

Date: _____

© Claire Jamieson and Ellen Morgan (2008) *Managing Dyslexia at University*, Oxon: Routledge

Student Questionnaire

This questionnaire should be completed by students who have either been previously assessed as having dyslexia and require a top-up assessment, or by students who are requesting a diagnosis because of difficulties with literacy skills.

Name:	ID Number
Date of Birth:	Age in Years and Months:
Course:	Department:
Start Date:	Postgraduate/Undergraduate:
	Full/Part-time:
End Date:	Home/EU/Overseas:
Home Address:	Term-time Address:
Tel:	E-mail:

Date Completed:

© Claire Jamieson and Ellen Morgan (2008) *Managing Dyslexia at University*, Oxon: Routledge

NB This section is only for students who have had a previous assessment

What was the date of your last assessment?

How old were you at the time?

Was dyslexia diagnosed?

Do you have a copy of your report?

Were you granted extra time for GCSE and/or A-level examinations?

Have you applied for the DSA?

Stage of application: DSA already received : YES/NO
                               Awaiting response

NB This section is only for students who speak English as a second or additional language.

What is your first language?

How old were you when you started to learn English?

Did you receive your education through the medium of English?

What do you now consider to be your dominant language?

Do you consider yourself to be bilingual? YES/NO

Can you read and write in your first language? YES/NO

Did you have difficulty learning to read and spell in your first language? YES/NO

If Yes, give details:

© Claire Jamieson and Ellen Morgan (2008) *Managing Dyslexia at University*, Oxon: Routledge

The remainder of the form should be completed by all students, whether they have been assessed previously, have English as a first or additional language or have not been assessed before and are being 'screened' for a full assessment.

Medical History and Early Development

Were there any problems associated with your birth or early development?
If Yes, give details if known:

Do you have any history of hearing impairment?
If Yes, give details:

Have you had any serous illnesses or accidents?
If Yes, give details:

Do you know if any member of your family is dyslexic?
If Yes, give details:

Speech and Language Development

As a child, did you have any difficulty, or were you late in learning to talk?
Give details if known:

Did you receive speech and language therapy? YES/NO
If Yes, give details:

Do you have any speech or language problems now, e.g., pronunciation/oral expression? YES/NO
If Yes, give details:

Education

When you first went to school, did you have difficulty learning to read?	YES/NO
Have you always had difficulty with spelling?	YES/NO
Have you ever had extra tuition to develop your literacy skills? If Yes, give details:	YES/NO
Do you still have reading/spelling difficulties?	YES/NO
Did you have difficulty learning languages at school?	YES/NO

© Claire Jamieson and Ellen Morgan (2008) *Managing Dyslexia at University*, Oxon: Routledge

Examinations

GCSE, CSE or O level

Subject	GCSE/CSE etc.	Grade	Date
English language			
Foreign language			

A level or equivalent

Subject	Grade	Date

Other qualifications (including degrees, BTec, NVQ, Access courses)

Subject	Course	Where taken	Date

Assessment

Have you ever had an assessment for dyslexia?	YES/NO
If so, do you have a copy of your report?	YES/NO
When did the assessment take place?	Date:
Was dyslexia diagnosed?	YES/NO
Did you have extra time in GCSE/A-level examinations?	YES/NO

Current Difficulties

Outline the problems you are experiencing with study and literacy skills, for example, reading or spelling difficulties, planning written assignments, expressing ideas coherently orally and in writing, handwriting legibility and speed. When did you first become aware that you had these difficulties?

© Claire Jamieson and Ellen Morgan (2008) *Managing Dyslexia at University*, Oxon: Routledge

Dyslexia Tuition Record Form

STUDENT	
COURSE	
E-MAIL	
PHONE	

YEAR OF STUDY		DSA Funding body State local authority/NHS etc. (if eligible)	

DATE	FROM	TO	LENGTH OF TUITION	STUDENT SIGNATURE
	TOTAL HOURS			

TUTOR'S NAME: _____

TUTOR'S SIGNATURE: _____ DATE: _____

© Claire Jamieson and Ellen Morgan (2008) *Managing Dyslexia at University*, Oxon: Routledge

UNIVERSITY LOGO/
LETTERHEAD

DYSLEXIA/DISABILITY SERVICES

Dyslexia Tuition Evaluation Form

Name of Student:

Course/Year:

Date, Time and Length of Session:

Session number:

Focus of Session (e.g., note-taking, essay-planning, revision/exam techniques):

Strategies Introduced:

Learning Outcomes:

Students' View of Session

Plans for Next Session:

Date of Next Session:

© Claire Jamieson and Ellen Morgan (2008) *Managing Dyslexia at University*, Oxon: Routledge

References

Bradley, L. and Bryant, P. (1983) 'Categorising Sounds and Learning to Read: A Causal Connection', *Nature*, 301: 419–21.

Byrne, B. (1998) *The Foundations of Literacy: The Child's Acquisition of the Alphabetic Principle*, Hove: Psychology Press.

Defries, J. C., Alarcon, M. and Olson, R. K. (1997) 'Genetic Etiologies of Reading and Spelling Deficits: Developmental Differences', in C. Hulme, and M. J. Snowling (eds) *Dyslexia: Biology, Cognition and Intervention*, London: Whurr, pp. 20–37.

DfES, now DIUS (1991) *The National Numeracy Strategy: Guidance to Support Pupils with Dyslexia and Dyscalculia*, London: DfES.

DIUS, formerly DfES (2007) *Bridging the Gap: A Guide to the Disabled Students' Allowances in Higher Education*, London: DIUS.

Ehri, L. C. (1995) 'Phases of Development in Learning to Read Words by Sight', *Journal of Research in Reading*, 18: 116–25.

Evans, B. (2001) *Dyslexia and Vision*, London: Whurr.

Frederickson, N. and Reason, R. (1995) 'Discrepancy Definitions of Specific Learning Difficulties', *Educational Psychology in Practice*, 10: 3–12.

Gillberg, C. (1991) 'Clinical and Eurobiological Aspects of Asperger Syndrome in Six Family Studies', in U. Frith (ed.), *Autism and Asperger Syndrome*, Cambridge: Cambridge University Press.

Goswami, U. and Bryant, P. (1990) *Phonological Skills and Learning to Read*, London: Lawrence Erlbaum.

Goulandris, N. (2003) *Dyslexia in Different Languages: Cross-linguistic Comparisons*. London: Whurr.

Grigorenko, E. L., Wood, F. B., Meyer, M. S., Hart, L. A., Speed, W. C., Shuster, A. and Pauls, D. L. (1997) 'Susceptibility Loci for Distinct Components of Developmental Dyslexia on Chromosomes 6 and 15, *American Journal of Human Genetics*, 60: 27–39.

Howe, M. A. J. (1997) *IQ in Question: The Truth about Intelligence*, London: Sage.

Hulme, C. and Roodenrys, S. (1995) Practitioner Review. Verbal working memory development and its disorders. *Journal of Child Psychology and Psychiatry*, 36:373–398.

Irlen, H. (1983) 'Successful treatment of learning disabilities.' Paper presented at the 91st Annual Convention of the American Psychological, Anaheim, Ca.

Irlen, H. (1991) *Reading by the Colors*, New York: Avery.

Jamieson, J. and Jamieson, C. (2004) *Managing Asperger Syndrome at College and University*, London: David Fulton.

Jamieson, C. and Jamieson, J. (2003) *Manual for Testing and Teaching English Spelling*, London: Whurr.

Jamieson, C. and Simpson, S. (2006) 'Spelling: Challenges and Strategies for the Teacher' in M. Snowling, and J. Stackhouse (eds), *Dyslexia Speech and Language*, 2nd ed., London: Whurr, pp. 198–228.

Miles, T. R. (1996) 'Do Dyslexic Children have IQs?' *Dyslexia*, 2 (3): 175–8.

Morgan, E. (2005) 'ADSHE: Uniting Dyslexia Specialists in Higher Education' in S. Tresman and A. Cooke (eds), *The Dyslexia Handbook*, Reading: British Dyslexia Association, pp. 195–9.

Morgan, E., Burn, E. and Pioli, L. (2000) 'Three Perspectives on Supporting a Dyslexic Trainee Teacher', *Innovations in Education and Training International*, 37 (2): 172–7.

Morgan, E. and Klein, C. (2000) *The Dyslexic Adult in a Non-Dyslexic World*, London: Whurr.

Morgan, W. (1997) 'Dyslexia and Combating Ignorance', *Probation Journal*, 44 (3): 132–9.

Mortimore, T. (2003) *Dyslexia and Learning Style: A Practitioner's Handbook*, London: Whurr.

Muter, V. (2003) *Early Reading Development and Dyslexia*, London: Whurr.

Pennington, B. F., Orden, G. C. V., Smith, S. D., Green, P. A. and Haith, M. M. (1990) 'Phonologcal Processing Skills and Deficits in Adult Dyslexics', *Child Development*, 61: 1753–78.

Royal College of Nursing (2005) 'Guidance for Mentors of Learner Nurses and Midwives', available online at <http://www.rcn.org.uk/publications/pdf/guidance_for_mentors.pdf>.

Siegel, L. S. (1999) 'Issues in the Definition and Diagnosis of Learning Disabilities', *Journal of Learning Disabilities*, 32 (4): 304–19.

Singleton, C. (Chair) (1999) *Dyslexia in Higher Education: Policy, Provision and Practice (Report of the National Working Party on Dyslexia in Higher Education)* Hull: University of Hull.

Smith, S. D., Kimberling, W. J., Pennington, B. F. and Lubs, H. A. (1983) 'Specific Reading Disability: Identification of and Inherited Form through Linkage Analysis', *Science*, 219: 1345–7.

Snowling, M. J. and Hulme, C. (1994) 'The Development of Phonological Skills', *Philosophical Transactions of the Royal Society*, 346 (B): 21–8.

Snowling, M. J., Nation, K., Moxham, P., Gallagher, A. and Frith, U. (1997) 'Phonological Processing Deficits in Dyslexic Students: A Preliminary Account', *Journal of Research in Reading*, 20: 31–4.

Stackhouse, J. (1992) 'Developmental Verbal Dyspraxia 1: A Review and Critique', *European Journal of Disorders of Communication*, 27 (1): 19–34.

Stanovich, K. E. (1986) Explaining the romance in reading ability in terms of psychological processes: what have we learned? *Annals of Dyslexia*, 35:67–96.

Stanovich, K. E. (1991) 'Discrepancy Definitions of Reading Disability: Has Intelligence Led us Astray?' *Reading Research Quarterly*, 26: 7–29.

Stanovich, K. E. and Stanovich, P. J. (1997) 'Further Thoughts on Aptitude/Achievement Discrepancy', *Educational Psychology in Practice*, 13 (1): 3–8.

Wilkins, A. J. (2002) 'Coloured Overlays and their Effects on Reading Speed: A Review', *Opthalmology, Physiology, Optometry*, 22: 448–54.

Wilkins, A. J., Huang, J. and Cao, Y. (2004) 'Visual Stress Theory and its Application to Reading and Reading Tests', *Journal of Research in Reading*, 27 (2): 152–62.

Websites

Note: all websites correct on 1 February 2007.

Academic support for dyslexic students
www.bbk.ac.uk/disability/resources/dyslexia

ADSHE
www.adshe.org.uk

Adult Dyslexia Organisation
www.futurenet.co.uk/charity/ado/adomenu/adomenu.htm

Asperger Syndrome
www.autism.org.uk

The British Dyslexia Association
www.bdadyslexia.org.uk

DDIG (Dyscalculia and Dyslexia Interest Group)
ddig.lboro.ac.uk

Department for Children, Schools and Families (DSCF, formerly DfES)

www.dcsf.gov.uk

Department for Innovation, Universities and Skills (DIUS, formerly DfES)

www.dius.gov.uk

The Disability Rights Commission
www.drc-gb.org/

Disabled Students' Allowances
www.direct.gov.uk/en/DisabledPeople/EducationandTraining/HigherEducation

Dyscalculia

- www.bbc.co.uk/skillswise/tutors/expertcolumn/dyscalculia/
- www.bbc.co.uk/skillswise/tutors/expertcolumn/dyslexia/index.shtml
- www.dfes.gov.uk/readwriteplus/understandingdyslexia/introduction/
  whatdoweknowaboutdyscalculia (Department for Education and Skills).

Dyslexia Action (formerly The Dyslexia Institute)
www.dyslexiaaction.org.uk

Dyspraxia
www.dyspraxiafoundation.org.uk

International Dyslexia Association (IDA)
www.interdys.org

London Language and Literacy Unit
www.lsbu.ac.uk/lllu

Neurodiversity
www.brainhe.com/index.html

PATOSS
www.patoss-dyslexia.org

Placements

- (Best Practice Guide: disabled social work students and placements) PedDS Project: www.hull.ac.uk/pedds
- National Network of Assessment Centres www.nnac.org/index.html

SKILL National Bureau for Students with Disabilities
www.skill.org.uk

Technology and dyslexia

- www.techdis.ac.uk
- www.dyslexic.com

Other Resources

Backhouse, G. and Morris, K. (eds) (2005) *Dyslexia Assessing and Reporting: The Patoss Guide*, London: Hodder Murray.

Burns, Tom and Sinfield, Sandra (2003) *Essential Study Skills: The Complete Guide to Success at University*, London: Sage Study Skills.

Butterworth, Brian (1999) *What Counts: How Every Brain is Hardwired for Math*, New York: Free Press.

Cottrell, S. (2003) *The Study Skills Handbook*, Basingstoke: Palgrave Macmillan.

Crystal, D. (2004) *Rediscover Grammar*, London: Longman.

Farmer, M., Riddick, B. and Sterling, C. (2002) *Dyslexia and Inclusion: Assessment and Support in Higher Education*, London: Whurr.

Goodwin, Vicki and Thomson, Bonita (2004) *Making Dyslexia Work for You: A Self-Help Guide*, London: David Fulton.

Hunter-Carsch, M. and Herrington, M. (2001) *Dyslexia and Effective Learning in Secondary and Tertiary Education*, London: Whurr.

Krupska, M. and Klein, C. (1995) *Demystifying Dyslexia*, London: Language and Literacy Unit.

McLoughlin, D., Fitzgibbon, G. and Young, V. (1994) *Adult Dyslexia: Assessment, Counselling and Training*, London: Whurr.

McLoughlin, D., Leather, C. and Stringer, P. (2002) *The Adult Dyslexic: Interventions and Outcomes.* London, Whurr.

Morgan, B., Agobiani, S., Williams-Findlay, C., Owen Adams, J. (2006) *Supporting Students with Specific Learning Difficulties, Especially Dyslexia: A Discussion Document and Self-Assessment Framework for Universities*, Sunderland: University of Sunderland.

Pollak, David (2005) *Dyslexia, the Self and Higher Education: Learning Life Histories of Students Identified as Dyslexic*, Stoke-on-Trent: Trentham Books.

Riddick, B., Farmer, M. and Sterling, C. (1997) *Students and Dyslexia*, London: Whurr.

Royal College of Nursing (2005) *Guidance for Mentors of Learner Nurses and Midwives*, available online at <http://www.rcn.org.uk/publications/pdf/guidance_for_mentors.pdf>.

Scott, R. (2004) *Dyslexia and Counselling.* London: Whurr.

Skill (2006) 'NMC Consultation on Proposals Arising from a Review of Fitness for Practice at the Point of Registration', available online at <http://www.skill.org.uk/news/policy/word/Nursing_&_Midwifery>.

Index

academic: assessment *see* marking; framework 70; standards 48, 49; tutor 65
Access to Learning Fund (ALF) 14, 63, 69
accreditation of prior experience (APE) 13
accreditation of prior learning (APL) 13
acquired dyslexia 1
alphabetic principle 38
alphabetic/non-alphabetic languages 1, 45
amanuensis 53
Asperger Syndrome **6**, 9, 70
assessment: diagnostic 8–16, *see also* diagnosis; tools *see* tests
Associate Membership of the British Dyslexia Association (AMBDA) 12, 13
Association for Dyslexia Specialists in Higher Education (ADSHE) 13, **22**
Attention Deficit Disorder (ADD) **5**, 70
Attention Deficit Hyper-Activity Disorder (ADHD) **5**, 9, 70
auditory working memory 9, 39, 44 *see also* short term memory; working memory

Bridging the Gap 28, 31
British Dyslexia Association (BDA) 12
British Psychological Society (BPS) 13

causes and effects of dyslexia 3
Code of Practice 1994 17, 24
Code of Practice 1999 48
Code of Practice 2006 48
cognitive processing 9, 12
compensatory strategies 9
competence standards 18, 21, 37, 44, **48–9**
comprehension 35
computer use in examinations 52
concentration 35
confidential information 69

confidentiality 14, 57; *see also* disclosure; confidential information
Continuing Professional Development (CPD) 13
coursework 15, 18, 49, 54

decoding 34; *see also* reading
definition of dyslexia 2
degree subject choice 18
Department for Education and Skills (DfES) (DIUS) 6, 8, 10, 11, 22, 27–9
developmental dyslexia 1–2
diagnosis: of dyslexia 3; late diagnosis of dyslexia 4
diagnostic: assessor 63; criteria **8–9**, 10
digital recorders 40, 56
disability 24–7; coordinator 57; equality schemes 26; services 60
Disability Discrimination Act (DDA) 17, 24–6; *see also* SENDA
Disability Equality Duty 26
Disability Rights Commission (DRC) 26, 48
Disabled Students' Allowances (DSA) 8, 17, **27–31**, 55, 58
disclosure **57**, 69
discrepancy 3, **9**
discrimination 26
dyscalculia **6**, 70
Dyslexia Action 12, 13
Dyslexia: coordinator 22, 49, 57, **62**; tutors *see* learning support; specialist teachers
dyspraxia 4, 9, 40, 45, 60, 70

eligibility for DSA *see* DSA
English as a second or additional language 10
encoding *see* spelling
examination arrangements 51–4, 66

examinations 44; extra time 44, 51
expressive language difficulties 43

feedback 22, 37, 39, 50
flagging 54
foreign languages 44; *see also* second languages; English as a second or additional language
funding for assessments 14, **29**, 63

genetic/neurological basis for dyslexia 1
glossaries 36

handouts 40, 41
Helen Arkell Dyslexia Centre (HADC) 13
Higher Education Funding Council in England (HEFCE) 25–6
Higher Education Statistics Agency (HESA) 22

information processing 38, 51
intelligence 3, **9**, 10 *see also* IQ; underlying ability
International Dyslexia Association (IDA) 2
international students 67; DSA 58
Irlen Syndrome *see* Scotopic Sensitivity Syndrome
IQ 3

label (dyslexia) 27
language of mathematics *see* mathematical language
learning/language support services 70
learning support 54, 64, 70
lectures 56; placements 56–7
lectures *see* note-taking; *see also* reasonable adjustments
library 55; staff 27, 55
literacy skills 8, 12, 20
local authorities 17, 28
London Language and Literacy Unit (LLLU+) 13

marking 21, 37, 39
mathematical language 42
Meares-Irlen Syndrome *see* Scotopic Sensitivity Syndrome
mind-mapping 41, 50

motor: clumsiness 6, *see also* dyspraxia; coordination 4; *see also* motor clumsiness *and* dyspraxia; skills 40; *see also* dyspraxia

National Committee for Standards in Assessment, Training and Practice (SASC) 13
National Health Service (NHS) Student Grants Unit (SGU) 28, 31
needs: assessment 14, 29; assessors 30, 31; reports 29
non-alphabetic languages 45
non-medical helper's allowance 64
note-taking 2, 38, **40–2**
number skills 42

Open University 28
opportunities for learning 9
oral skills *see* expressive language difficulties
organisational difficulties 5

personal tutor 27, 65
phonemes 2
phonics 2
phonological: awareness 2; processing 2, 9, 11, 12, 43
placements *see* reasonable adjustments
plagiarism 21, 42
postgraduate students 30
practising certificate 12
presentations *see* expressive language difficulties
Professional Association for Teachers of Learners with SpLD (PATOSS) 8, 12, 13
psychologists 12
punctuation 21, 37

qualifications 8, **12**
Quality Assurance Agency (QAA) 48
Quality Assurance Group (QAG) 30
questionnaire 70

reader *see* examination arrangements
reading 12, **34–6**
reasonable adjustments 25, 37, **48–59**; examinations 51–4; coursework 54–5
reassessment 10

recommendations 12, 29
recording lectures 41; *see also* digital recorders
registration form 69
report (diagnostic assessment) 14, 29, 31
report format 8, 12
resources 69
roles and responsibilities 60–7
rote learning 2

SASC *see* National Committee for Standards in Assessment Training and Practice
Scotopic Sensitivity Syndrome 5
screening 11
second languages 8; *see also* English as an additional or second language
self esteem 14, 25
short term memory 11, 39; *see also* auditory working memory; visual memory
sight vocabulary 34, 35
software 30, 52 *see also* technology
spatial ability 3
Special Educational Needs Disability Act (SENDA) 17, 22, 25, 48, 61; *see also* DDA
specialist: equipment *see* technology; teachers 12, 13, 22, 27, 49 *see also* learning support; tutors *see* specialist teacher *and* learning support
specific learning difficulties 4
speech sounds 2; *see also* phonemes; phonology; phonological awareness; phonological processing

spelling 12, 21, **37–9**; non-phonetic 38; strategies 39
software *see* technology
spoonerism test 10
Student Loan Company 28
study skills support *see* specialist teachers; learning support
subject tutors 27; *see also* academic tutor
support tutors *see* specialist teachers; learning support

technology 29–30; training 30, 31
tests: standardised, open, closed 11
time management 6, 45
tuition *see* specialist teachers *and* learning support; evaluation 70; record 70

underlying ability 12
University and Colleges Admissions Service (UCAS) 61

Visual: discomfort *see* Scotopic Sensitivity Syndrome; memory 9; processing 12
viva voce examinations 43, 49

widening participation 17
word finding difficulties 43
working memory 2, 12, 35 *see also* auditory working memory; short term memory; visual memory
writing 12, **37–8**; speed 40

Library Use Only